High Grade Living

From the founders of The Broad Place,
Jacqui Lewis & Arran Russell

High
Grade
Living

A guide to creativity,
clarity and mindfulness

For our daughter, Marley,
our queen of high-grade living

First published in Australia in 2020
by Thames & Hudson Australia Pty Ltd
11 Central Boulevard, Portside Business Park
Port Melbourne, Victoria 3207
ABN: 72 004 751 964

thamesandhudson.com.au

Thames & Hudson Australia wishes to acknowledge that Aboriginal and Torres Strait
Islander people are the first storytellers of this nation and the traditional custodians
of the land on which we live and work. We acknowledge their continuing culture and
pay respect to Elders past, present and future.

978 1 7607603 4 2

A catalogue record for this
book is available from the
National Library of Australia

NATIONAL LIBRARY OF AUSTRALIA

Every effort has been made to trace accurate ownership of copyrighted text and
visual materials used in this book. Errors or omissions will be corrected in subsequent
editions, provided notification is sent to the publisher.

Front and back cover photos: Arran Russell
Design: Arran Russell
Typesetting: Megan Ellis
Editing: Brigid James
Printed and bound in China by C&C Offset Printing Co., Ltd

FSC® is dedicated to the promotion of responsible forest management
worldwide. This book is made of material from FSC®-certified forests and
other controlled sources.

MIX
Paper from
responsible sources
FSC® C008047

How We Found
Our Broad Place

In the frenzy of modern life, many of us have lost our path. With so much external influence, we have attempted to build a version of ourselves from the outside in, rather than from the inside out. Influenced by so many people, circumstances and experiences, we have brought a lot of what isn't true to us into our personal architecture.

I have spent decades studying all that I could access and discover in meditation, Vedic knowledge, Buddhism, Zen, Taoism, yoga, karate, tai chi, qi gong, Ayurveda, nutrition, neuroscience and science. I have always tried to push the boundaries of knowledge and techniques to see what might work. They all led me in the right direction, and in fact all these disciplines are saying the same thing at their core: that the truth of us lies within us, and cannot be found outside of us. That there is a natural intelligence connecting all things that we can access and live in alignment with, and that starts with our hearts.

After ten years of learning so many meditation techniques that didn't really stick, I finally came across what I now teach: a twenty-minute, twice-daily practice of mind transcendence with a mantra. I enthusiastically recommended it to everyone at first. But this was around a decade ago, before meditation was clearly communicated by the world's top thinkers, actors, creatives and corporates as the most important thing they practise and so was being largely resisted in the West. I was often mystified by people thinking you had to become vegan or only wear linen or not drink alcohol to meditate. You can meditate and still live however you want. Arran, my husband, collaborator and co-founder of The Broad Place, also learned this meditation technique after a tonne of initial resistance, and was practising every day. It was life-changing for both of us.

Our friend James came up with the term 'the broad place' with his mother when she was undergoing rigorous cancer treatments. They would experience these moments when clarity would break through all the fear, pain and anxiety. There was a sense of absolute trust and a deep knowledge that everything was going to be okay, no matter what happened. There was no thinking in these broad moments, just simple being. James and I used to speak deeply about how these moments shaped us, the experience of being in complete flow, trusting, and moving from the heart and not the head. I became obsessed with accessing this deeper, true part of myself, with not just finding my broad place, but taking up full-time residence there.

In utter peace, and with contentment and a sense of complete unity amid chaos, I would have these extraordinary breakthroughs as I found my own broad places in the chaos of my life as a mother, wife and owner of multiple businesses. Within my meditation practice and outside of it, I started to experience deep states of absolute joy with much more frequency. It might be 2 am, and I would come home after launching a client's new restaurant or brand, shatteringly exhausted – the kind of fatigue where your bones ache. With this physical burn, I would walk up the stairs in our spookily dark terrace house, and Marley, our young daughter, would be asleep in her bed with the window open so the moon shone on her. Her little child hair would wisp about her soft cheeks, and in the still of night I would stand and watch her sleep, filled with worried thoughts about the event, her, my parenting, my business. She used to do this thing where she would stay asleep, but it was as though she could sense my presence, and she would take a huge breath in and then sigh long and soft. All my thoughts and worry would instantly vanish, and I would stand there with the deepest sense of connection and overwhelming love, and not a single thought. This would sometimes also happen when I dived into the ocean and floated on my back, in absolute awe of what it felt like to be alive. Sometimes it was seeing a bird fly overhead in the dusk. Sometimes simply making eye contact with Arran across a crowded room. It was like time would stop, warp and expand, and the presence of that moment was almost overwhelming. On occasion I would burst into tears from such an overflow of beauty, of what it meant to be alive, before snapping back into normal thinking and life.

These moments kept increasing in frequency and volume. It felt like touching a truth. I became determined to access my broad place more deeply by letting go of all the things that didn't help me experience this. I also wanted others to be able to experience their broad place, and that coincided with Arran and I reaching a particular tipping point in our lives.

At this time, we were working like crazy across so many businesses, living in the eastern suburbs of Sydney, and our

High-Grade Living

daughter was about to start school. Like so many, we were very adept at the 'doing' in life, highly skilled and overworked. Arran owned a men's fashion brand and had just won *GQ Australia* Designer of the Year. We had a very successful waterfront restaurant and cafe. We also ran a creative communications agency where we worked with luxury and boutique clients on their design work, advertising and marketing, as well as events and experiences. Arran had an award-winning vodka brand he created and produced in the Czech Republic on the side. We were overworked and burnt out, surrounded by people who were somehow even more burnt out than we were. Within all this doing and its resulting success, we had a sense that something was still missing.

I started to chat with Arran about a place, a school, in which people who weren't necessarily into 'spirituality', but wanted to evolve, could learn in an environment of equality. A place in which you didn't have to subscribe to eating a certain way, looking a certain way, or even more annoyingly, speaking with certain jargon and getting a new name. A place where you weren't judged by your choices, but where diversity was celebrated and education could be approached by anyone from anywhere in a clean and clear way. It was through this that I became very clear about what I could potentially contribute as a meditation teacher, by stripping out the smoke and mirrors, dogma and spiritual bypassing that frequently defined meditation in the West.

In essence, our livelihoods had been based on the art of convincing and providing people with a purchase, a product, an experience to supply happiness from outside of themselves, and hopefully getting them hooked on it. What we discovered though was that most people, ourselves included, were consuming to fill a hole, or to justify why we worked so hard in the first place. Having said that, we still believe that there is nothing wrong with consumerism if it is thoughtful and in alignment with our values. We don't think that in order to access our higher selves we need to live Gandhi-style with only seven possessions. What we do believe is that when we lose the place within our hearts that tells us what's real, what's important and what's true for us, it is time to come back to ourselves.

The Broad Place was formed as a school to get in touch with your being, to come into contact with your higher self, the truth

opposite, top left *Our daughter, Marley, with Arran, travelling with us while I taught. She has joined us and assisted on so many retreats, including in India, and has been a delight to have around as The Broad Place has grown. She has seen her fair share of students go through deep experiences and has always been so kind and sweet to all of them.*

opposite, top right *Arran and I at our pink house in Palm Beach, Sydney, Australia.*

opposite, bottom *The Broad Place Paddington School in Sydney set up for evenings of meditation and knowledge.*

of yourself, as a creative and conscious human. This journey is not about acquisition as much as it is about removing what's not working, with attention to all the things that have been unconsciously added. Some dismantling, renovation and shifting of our beliefs, values and ways of being helps us begin to live in alignment with our hearts again, as we naturally did as children. When we were young, our intuition tuned in deeply, we inherently knew how to *be* as humans. Then we were taught the importance of 'doing' in life – action, goals and models of success. It is through all this doing that our sense of self can get lost. Your broad place is where you return to your true self.

High-grade living is the term we have created to explain this process, living in alignment with our higher selves. When we refer to high-grade paper or a high-grade textile, we understand that it means refinement, bringing the best to the world. It's as much about saying no to certain things as it is about saying yes. We can take the same approach to ourselves through high-grade living, removing anything that does not align with our true selves and inviting in the things that do. 'High grade' doesn't mean a ladder-style system, where we climb the ranks of our minds and consciousness. It's simply about you discovering and embracing what is you, and letting go of what is not.

Creating The Broad Place was a terrifying time, as I was still managing all our other businesses and my family. I had no idea if we could make this idea of a school work. What if no one else desired what we did? Were we absolutely kidding ourselves? I was no monk and never wanted to be a guru. What I did want was to teach techniques that I knew worked. But would anyone else want an authentic, brutally honest, person-on-the-ground approach to teaching? Or did people actually want hierarchy, a guy in a robe with mala beads and feelings of exclusivity? Our teachings were outcome-based. They would come from time-honoured truths and practical experience, and focus on improving the quality of life for our students, teachers and community. But we had no idea if this was what people actually wanted.

I truly think that without the clarity we received from meditation, The Broad Place would not have been created. It was this clarity that in turn gave us the confidence to found The Broad Place. After founding, The Broad Place grew like a

top left *Arran and I with our tintype portraits by Jeff Kober, photographer, actor and meditation teacher.*

bottom right *Food as a shared experience is at the centre of what we create for our retreats and longer events. Whether cooking myself or working with chefs, including my dad, Greg Doyle, over the years, it has been a joy and delight. Breaking down barriers over a shared meal is transformative.*

High-Grade Living

How We Found Our Broad Place

High-Grade Living

wildfire, globally. We were travelling all around the world to teach meditation, and set up a permanent school in Australia, where people from around the country and all over the world came to study. We were totally committed to creating high-grade education, experiences and products, and every element was turned over, assessed and refined. It became a live philosophy experiment, where our thinking infused every component. I think this, combined with our passion for creativity, process and sequence after decades of working in creative industries, gave us a deep appreciation for what we were doing. The foundation of all we shared was a response to these questions: Do we love this? Do we know that it will work? Is it beautiful? Arran and I both believe that beauty, from nature and all the objects that we surround ourselves with, makes the heart sing.

There is no hierarchy within The Broad Place, and all teachers and students are treated equally. We are not a personality-driven organisation. We are very wary of creating 'gurus', recognising that this concept can become distorted and abused. We are also on guard for the human tendency to 'disciple' and place teachers on a pedestal, and instead encourage students to determine their own truths through the practical teachings we provide. This has set us on solid foundations. As a global school we are committed to creating a new paradigm for education and self-development, celebrating creativity and consciousness.

This begs the question: if it's all within us, deep in our hearts, why do we need any help at all? If what we hope to discover – more creativity, clarity, consciousness and peace – is already there, why don't we simply tap into it? Arran and I have travelled the world, studying, learning and experiencing, to answer this very question. The Broad Place is a culmination of years upon years of experimenting, refining, letting go, layering in. Like a human guinea pig, I have taken these findings and shared them with students.

This book could have been ten times longer and deeper, so we had to choose carefully what to include. Arran and I have been together almost a decade and within this time have systematically and spontaneously experimented with every area of life. There have been some hilarious moments and some very trying periods. Creating The Broad Place hasn't been a gentle, easy

previous pages, top right *Marley and Arran in Japan.*

previous pages, bottom right *Dinner with friends in Japan.*

opposite, top left *The incredible Emily Snape, who has been a part of the Broad Place family for years now, first assisting me on every project and then becoming an Integrated Meditation teacher. I can't explain how much I adore her.*

opposite, top right *Emily with Toofy, our fifteen-year-old rescue dog who has no teeth after experiencing a decade of neglect before we got him. He loves Emily's beautiful energy.*

opposite, bottom *Staying curious is how we've always tried to live: eyes wide, heart open, delighted at the world around us.*

path. It's been hot, sweaty work, emotionally turbulent; a rapid learning curve that has often felt like falling face-first down the side of a mountain. There have been endless disappointments, frustrations and learnings. But there has also been joy, excitement, creativity and connection in equal measure. This is all part of taking people on huge personal journeys – not just to places like India, but deep within themselves.

This book will help you begin that inner work, and outer work, to access and live from your broad place. How do you take all of this knowledge and experience and put it into a book? We felt that a sort of manual might be the answer, with a balance among philosophy, practice, techniques and prompts for action. I have always wanted shoulder-to-shoulder, on-the-ground teachings, experiences and learnings, and that is what we hope to share with you here.

All the learnings and experiences from both of us, and our students from Sydney to Jaipur, Osaka, Los Angeles, Hong Kong, Berlin and beyond, have shaped the words, tools and philosophies within this book. They are tried and tested. We believe this is ultimately the key – integrating knowledge into practice. Pushing it, pulling it and working out what bits fit us as individuals. We all know deep down that a cookie-cutter approach doesn't work; yet we all crave a simple ten-step list on how to live our lives. This book is not going to tell you what to do, but instead arm you with the tools to discover what works for you. Some ideas will delight you, and some simply won't work for you. It's about you discovering and embracing what is you, and letting go of what is not.

The chapter on Diving into Meditation is not a guide on how to meditate as an experienced meditator, but inspiration and instruction on building a practice, finding a teacher, and what you can experience from meditation. There are helpful rituals to enhance a meditation practice as well as a beginner's breath meditation for those who want to dip their toes in immediately.

The chapter on Your Home as a Retreat is overflowing with ideas and styles of living. Arran and I have shifted around Sydney from an apartment in a residential area, to a flat on the ocean, to a tall and narrow terrace house, to a sprawling home, to a tiny cottage surrounded by nature, to a huge home on the beach surrounded by trees, and now to an apartment in London. We gave

opposite The experience of gathering to share philosophy and stories is prevalent in every culture, and this is a cornerstone of The Broad Place. The shared experience is a powerful one, and for many of our students, The Broad Place is one of the only places where they can connect with people interested in elevating themselves through greater clarity, creativity and consciousness, so it becomes a sacred space. This is River Hawk Ranch in Byron Bay, Australia, where many special gatherings have taken place.

following pages, left *The view from the top of the headland at Palm Beach in Sydney, Australia, down to our home, as seen on our morning walks.*

following pages, right *Arran and I in the Broad Place Paddington studio in Sydney.*

High-Grade Living

High-Grade Living

How We Found Our Broad Place

High-Grade Living

away and sold almost all that we owned so we could answer the question: do we own our things, or do they own us? We have had to decide what brought us joy, why the home was so important, and deliberately create and then re-create how we lived. In this chapter we have tried to include as many practical tips as possible, so that you can experiment for yourself.

The Expanding Your Creativity chapter has a thick thread of curiosity running through it. We invite you to drop all your prejudices and explore and acknowledge your individual creativity. Arran and I have been creating since we were little children – not just art, but businesses and experiences – and our thirst for learning still grows.

The Deepening Your Relationships chapter is a series of prompts that you can use to explore how you relate to yourself and to the world. It includes many exercises you can do to help you establish how your words and actions reflect who you are. There are lots of journal prompts and ways to experiment with the learnings from journaling. I wanted it to be a personal dive into what makes you tick and what makes you light up.

Years ago I was explaining to one of my students – Danielle, a composer – the meaning behind The Broad Place. I described those beautiful breakthrough moments amid all the noise of being human, when you know, at your core, what it means to be whole and alive, to feel completely expanded and broad. She sighed deeply and said, 'Oh yes, it's the same as music.' She went on to explain that most people think music is primarily the notes and their sequencing. But music is also the gaps between the notes, the tiny pockets of silence and stillness. This is what her meditation practice was to her: gaps punctuating the noise and activity of her day. And surrounded by these little moments of stillness, the activity became more beautiful, more of a symphony.

The broad place is what it means to have gaps in between, to be in contact with the truth of ourselves – to be expansive instead of contracted, in our love, our creativity, our actions, our thinking and, most importantly, our being. We have kept the imagery in this book raw and real to inspire you on your path to authenticity. We hope this book helps you to create your high-grade life, to find your broad place and take up residence there.

—Jacqui Lewis, 2019

opposite *I grew up in Palm Beach, on the Northern Beaches of Sydney, Australia, and have returned time and time again. It is a place of immense healing for our family and transformation for The Broad Place. Arran and I would wake and walk our dogs at sunrise daily on this beach, seeing dolphins often and talking through all that we were planning and creating. It was a moment in our day when dreams were hatched, problems were shared and resolved, and we connected with nature and each other.*

'You deserve the best. Never feel unworthy or not justified in having the best. I tell you, this is your heritage; but you have to accept it. You have to expect it; you have to claim it. To do so is not demanding too much.'

—Guru Deva

Diving into Meditation

We consider meditation to be the cornerstone of a high-grade life. When we are calm and centred, we understand everything better, including ourselves.

The Broad Place was founded to teach meditation to anyone who wanted to expand their life with more creativity, consciousness and clarity. Meditation is the bedrock of expansive thinking, and with a daily practice, the pathway to a high-grade life is that much more accessible. We have seen countless examples of sceptics being transformed into meditators.

But why does sitting still with your eyes closed when you have so much to do in your day help you become more productive? Our answer is that it's like exercise. When you're committed to an exercise routine, you may be using more energy, yet it trains your body to be more energetic. Not only that, but the happy hormones, the metabolic increase and the strength you gain from exercising also affect your mind, your mood and your brain for the better. Meditation works in exactly the same way. Pausing your action to just 'be' for a moment trains your body to bring you more energy and concentration in your day.

Not all meditation is the same. Our focus is on a mantra-based meditation practice where the mind dives into a deeper state of consciousness. This transcending technique comes from a long lineage, originating in India and stemming from Vedic knowledge. We call this technique Integrated Meditation, and it is taught in person by our teachers around the world.

'If, for example, you run around filling your mind with this and that, you will discover that your entire meditation is spent in letting go of the stuff you just finished collecting in the past few hours. You also notice that your meditations are clearer when you come into them from a simpler space. This encourages you to simplify your life.'

—Ram Dass

High-Grade Living

Understanding yourself

In the Western world today, meditation is used primarily as a method to reduce stress and fatigue, and increase productivity and clarity. These are all excellent reasons to meditate. However, in this book we're going to encourage you to go a little deeper.

Meditation can also be used as a path to understand yourself on a more profound level. When you know the truth about yourself and can reconcile that with your ideas about yourself and your adopted belief systems and values, you can begin the work of understanding others. Relating to people on a deeper level comes from knowing yourself first.

But how does meditation bring about this self-knowledge – especially when you feel like all you're doing is listening to the chatter in your head reminding you to send that email, pick up milk and clean the house? Learning to quieten that chatter is just one of the reasons that meditation is important.

While meditating, your body goes out of that fight-or-flight state and into rest and repair. This is vastly important for all people, and especially for busy, stressed people. From this calmer state, your mind and body begin to come together again. There is cohesion between the two that doesn't occur when you are rushing through your day.

A short history of meditation

Meditation originated in India over 5500 years ago and spread rapidly throughout the East over the following thousands of years via teachers travelling far and wide on foot. It is important to note that the challenge in documenting meditation is that it was taught person to person through oral traditions, and so the recorded dates of origin vary.

Initially the Vedas, religious texts originating in ancient India, were the centre of spirituality and meditation. These texts are thought to be where yoga, meditation and Ayurveda – an ancient Indian mind–body science used to balance and heal ourselves – all come from.

The word 'yoga' comes from a Sanskrit word meaning 'to yoke': unifying the mind and body. In the West, yoga now primarily refers to the practice of the movement and poses (the asanas) and is used for exercise as well as practising spiritual principles. However, exercise was not the original purpose of yoga. The asanas are only one part of a greater knowledge, philosophy and practice base. Yoga was used to achieve self-realisation, harmony of mind and body, and understanding of one's true nature. Meditation was originally an essential part of this. It was taught between teacher (*guru*) and student (*shishya*) in schools called *gurukuls*, and involved a monastic way of life. This tradition continues in the East today.

Meditation continued to expand into many countries, and the related philosophies became the foundation for religions such as Buddhism – thought to have spread from India into China and East Asia via the Buddhist monk Bodhidharma, and into Japan in a form called Zen.

As you learn more about meditation, you will find that many practices overlap with each other. There is no wrong way to meditate.

High-Grade Living

Meditation in the Western world

In the second half of the twentieth century, teachers of meditation from the East began to reach much greater numbers of people in the West, and their techniques and philosophies spread. This movement was pioneered by Indian gurus such as Maharishi Mahesh Yogi, Paramahansa Yogananda and Jiddu Krishnamurti, as well as by Westerners like British priest turned Zen practitioner Alan Watts and American Harvard professor turned spiritual teacher Ram Dass.

Possibly the most famous practitioners of meditation at this time were The Beatles, who studied Maharishi Mahesh Yogi's Transcendental Meditation technique in the 60s and 70s. Before long, meditation was being embraced in the West not only as a spiritual practice, but as an essential exercise to relieve the immense stress of that tumultuous era.

By the 90s, however, the attention meditation had been receiving in the West started to wane. The technological boom hit; meditation became associated with the hippies of a bygone era and seemed to have no place in a society that was becoming more and more interested in computers.

This technological progression has only snowballed in the last couple of decades, so why has meditation made such a comeback in the last ten years? It may simply be due to a combination of need, better education and easier access. The modern world is a challenging place, but greater understanding of anxiety and other mental health issues means that the stigma around seeking help is fast disappearing. People now look for alternative methods to deal with day-to-day stresses, and doctors all over the world are recommending meditation as a way to calm the nervous system and develop better mental health.

opposite *There are three primary types of meditation: concentration, contemplation and transcending. They are all created and practised differently, so finding a style that works for you and your lifestyle is important, as is not giving up after trying only one type. Not all meditation is the same, nor is just sitting still with your eyes closed meditation!*

The science behind meditation

Meditation can assist with a range of health issues, both physical and mental. It is used to help:

- reduce physical pain
- lower blood pressure
- improve anxiety and depression
- create better overall mental health
- improve sleep
- enhance cognitive functioning

In 2011, researchers at Massachusetts General Hospital reported the findings of a study on the impact of meditation on the brain. Following an eight-week mindfulness meditation program, the study found changes to the grey-matter density of participants' brains in areas linked to memory, self-awareness, compassion and stress. There is also evidence that regular meditation practice can keep a person's brain up to twenty years younger compared to the brains of people who don't meditate.

More than 35 million people in the US alone report having practised meditation, and it is only increasing in popularity. Our students claim that regular meditation has improved their creative thinking, confidence, decision-making and productivity. It has made them feel happier and more relaxed, and helped them become better parents and partners, and more compassionate and grateful members of society.

In essence, meditation is helping people achieve their full potential.

opposite, top left *The original aim of meditation was to reach enlightenment by looking deep within. Even for many of us who might not dedicate our lives to it, meditation can be a way to reach deeper inside of ourselves, to grow, to experience stillness in contrast to our busy lives.*

opposite, top right *The trees of Big Sur, California, USA, with their deep root systems and tall trunks: a reminder of how we meditate, at once deeply grounded and always growing.*

opposite, bottom left *You can meditate anywhere. This was a meditation I did in a huge gallery garden in Paris, France, captured on the sly by Arran.*

opposite, bottom right *A large group meditation and talk on creativity we held in a gallery with artist Joshua Yeldham. Connecting with fellow meditators is called a Sangha, and meditating in a group is a powerful experience that many students love.*

High-Grade Living

My first attempts at meditation

When I was a small child, I would often meditate. I loved sitting with my eyes closed and quietening down my mind.

I would do this at the beach, in a national park near our home or in the garden. Where I got this idea from is beyond me, as our family was far from being into meditation back then, and I can't remember seeing any books about it. However, the foundation was set. I started practising meditation more formally in the late 1990s, as a part of the yoga classes I was attending at the time.

This was before yoga was popular in the West, let alone trendy. There were no dedicated yoga schools, no fancy yoga fashion brands or social media showing people in extraordinary poses. My classes were held in a local hall and were considered, in general, rather an odd hobby. The meditation was very basic, but it reminded me deeply of the experiences I had as a child. This innocuous little yoga class launched my quest to try as many meditation techniques as I could, in search of something that would fit my lifestyle, my philosophy of life and my personal goals: emotional liberation and peace.

Since then – for the past twenty years – I have studied Buddhist, Taoist and many other Eastern philosophies; attended silent retreats; learned Kriya Yoga techniques; and trained in karate, qi gong and tai chi. My years of study have led me down a long and fruitful path to understanding that at their core, all of these philosophies point to the same teachings: that the mind and body must be aligned for harmony and peace, that we must look to nature for our answers, and that the energy underpinning everything is a single unified force.

The lineage I have explored most deeply is Vedic knowledge, with its fascinating teachings on yoga, meditation and Ayurveda. I first learned the transcending, mantra-based practice of Vedic meditation at a peak of stress and anxiety in my life. My years of intensive study have taken me around the world, to learn in many countries from many teachers. These learnings and daily practice have transformed my life – so much so that I committed to teaching the technique to others.

opposite *You can meditate absolutely anywhere and don't need to find an austere place to practise. Instead, try it wherever you can sit comfortably.*

following pages *We do like to create beautiful meditation experiences for our students, like this setting in Malibu, California, USA, that we set up for a special meditation gathering.*

My husband, Arran, had never meditated in his life and deeply resisted it for the first few years we were together. He rationalised that he wasn't 'stressed', so why would he meditate? It took a few years and some encouragement from friends to get him into daily Vedic meditation practice. He hadn't initially considered it as a technique to enhance his creativity and clarity, but once he started, he didn't want to stop. Meditation shifted the flow of our entire relationship, filling it with trust and shared experience.

When we established The Broad Place, we hoped to retain the tried and tested ancient mantras and practice of Vedic meditation, but deliver them in a way that was empathetic to people living modern lives. Sadly, as with most systems, hierarchy has always been present in meditation, and it has traditionally been a very patriarchal system. My aim has been to share meditation in an inclusive and creative way, separate from any outdated dogma. We refer to the main method that we teach and practise as Integrated Meditation: while still founded on the ancient transcending technique from the body of Vedic wisdom, it also draws on disciplines such as neuroscience, and lots of community support. Our focus is on people who want to elevate themselves through daily meditation practice and education so they can live with more clarity, creativity and consciousness.

opposite *Our home has always been an extension of our teaching, and here our house in Palm Beach, Sydney, Australia, is set up for a meditation gathering with students.*

Getting started

If you want to learn meditation, where do you begin? We feel that a basic background understanding of meditation, a brilliant teacher and a technique that works for you are what makes a person connect to meditation practice. If you haven't found a technique or teacher you like, keep looking. Meanwhile, you can practise on your own.

There are many myths and misconceptions surrounding meditation: people believe that it must be done in complete silence, that it requires you to live an ascetic life, and that it doesn't count unless you spend hours each day on it.

In reality, there are many ways you can practise meditation. Just like with exercise, not every meditation style is for everyone. Each method can differ greatly in terms of engagement, time and outcomes.

Finding a routine that suits you – and acknowledging that this may take some trial and error – is as important with meditation as it is with physical exercise. If you went for one run around the block and didn't immediately love it, it's unlikely you would then dismiss all kinds of exercise for the rest of your life, believing it simply isn't for you. Yet this is a common approach to meditation: people adopt the attitude of 'tried it once, couldn't do it' and then never have another go.

We encourage you to let go of all your preconceived ideas about meditation and start experimenting with practices that work for you.

There is much debate between traditionalists and innovators as to whether meditation should be taught online or only in person, but it really depends on the technique. At The Broad Place, we only teach Integrated Meditation in person, as we believe that's what works best for this method. However, there are also countless resources online and in books such as this one that can help you begin your meditation journey from the comfort of your own home.

Breath meditation

We recommend learning meditation in person with a teacher, rather than from a book. However, you can get started on your own with a beginner's style of meditation that is widely used, where the breath is the focal point.

Even though we're breathing all the time, we often forget to breathe deeply and properly in the course of our day. Breath meditation helps us centre ourselves and become completely aware and present.

right *Gardens like these are created as places of meditation and contemplation within the temples that are everywhere in Kyoto, Japan. We always think: Imagine what cities would be like if they all embraced meditation and created special places for people to meditate. What a shift in energy it would be.*

following pages *At home we often burn incense during meditation sittings, and the smoke wafting and curling in the air is a beautiful sight to open our eyes to at the end.*

High-Grade Living

Putting into practice

First, get yourself into a comfortable seated position. Sitting still is very important for this technique, so finding a way to sit comfortably is key.

Ideally, you should start breath meditation by sitting cross-legged on the floor, with your back straight. Some find it helpful to sit on a cushion to raise the buttocks off the ground and allow the legs to fall gently forward.

However, you may find that while sitting on the floor without a back support, you slump your back and shoulders. It's important to have a straight back, so we recommend sitting on a chair to begin with if you need that extra support. Experiment with both methods and find what works best for you.

Once seated, ensure that the spine is straight, the chin gently tucked in and the shoulders relaxed. Rest your hands comfortably and gently in your lap.

Close your eyes and become aware of your breathing. Your breaths should be light and easy, and gradually become longer in length.

Your breath is your guide during this meditation and it is what you come back to as an anchor for the busy mind.

Now move your focus to place your awareness on the lower belly. In Japanese practice this is known as the *hara*. Focus your mind intently there and breathe into this space. The belly should expand with each breath in and contract with each breath out. Each time you are distracted by thoughts (which will be constantly), this is the space you come back to.

As you concentrate on your breaths, the mind will dash about, the body will distract and surrounding noises will pester you. Don't worry; this is normal. When you find yourself distracted, simply come back to the breath. How does it feel in the body? Are the breaths long and slow, or are they shortening naturally? Bring your awareness back to the *hara* and your attention back to the breath.

Repeat this practice once or twice a day for 15 minutes. Routine is very important and will ground your practice.

top *When meditating, try to be as light as a cloud.*

bottom *I love tea ceremonies and have been learning through my friend Sam Gibb of Cloud Hidden and Global Tea Hut over the years. A tea ceremony brings such presence. It's a meditative state, although tea is not meditation alone. I like to preface my meditation sitting with a tea ceremony, as it enhances the experience so much. Our two rescue dogs, Toofy and Honey, are never far from us when we meditate or when we have tea; they pick up on the energy and love being around.*

Walking meditation

'We have to walk in a way that we only print peace and serenity on the earth…Walk as if you are kissing the earth with your feet.'

—Thich Nhat Hanh

Meditation is usually done seated with the eyes closed. However, meditative practices such as *kinhin* approach meditation in a different way. *Kinhin* in the Zen tradition is essentially mindful walking and is generally practised between long periods of seated meditation (*zazen*) or at the end of a *zazen* session. *Kinhin* is considered the thread that strings together a solid Zen practice. It's not only a welcome relief when practising hours-long sessions of seated Zen meditation, but also a beautiful awakening to the intricacies of movement.

You don't need to practise seated meditation to practise *kinhin*. It will calm you while helping you build a connection to the earth, leaving you grounded and at peace.

Putting into practice

To practise *kinhin*, make a gentle fist with your right hand, while bringing your left hand to gently cup your right. Your elbows should be relaxed but held out a little wider than normal. Ensure your spine is straight, your shoulders broad and your body relaxed. You should be looking down slightly, with your gaze heavy-lidded and soft.

When walking, each step is slow and careful, and you place your awareness on the feeling of your feet on the floor or ground, the air around you, your body's alignment and the position of your spine. Every physical sensation is gently acknowledged. Breath is soft, gentle and slow. You should be aware of each footstep, ball to toes, and the movement this sends through the body. Most *kinhin* is practised slowly, though I have seen practitioners in some monasteries move at a very fast pace. You may prefer a slow pace to start.

At the end of a *kinhin* session, palms are placed together in a traditional prayer position and the head and upper body gently bow. It is traditional to bow with gratitude.

Kinhin can be practised at any time of day. Mindfully walking with full attention on the body is a profound way of moving, and you can practise this outdoors or simply by going from room to room.

High-Grade Living

TIMING YOUR MEDITATION

We recommend finding a way to time your meditation without technology. Monasteries and ashrams use a gentle bell or wood block to announce the end of meditation. At The Broad Place, we love to use sand timers, which are a beautiful way to keep track of your practice. It's quite hard to avoid apps and alarms these days, but try removing them from your practice and work with a clock or watch instead, opening your eyes gently to check the time as you proceed. If you're worried about going over your allocated meditation time, set a buffer alarm a few minutes after the end time, so you don't run late but also aren't shocked out of your practice by an unnecessary noise.

above *In Zen traditions, gardens are symbols of presence and alignment to nature and are such remarkably beautiful places to be. I meditated overlooking this garden in Kyoto, Japan, and it's one I will always remember.*

Meditating with children

Now that we have put aside the idea that your meditation practice has to be done in a pristine, silent space, let's broach the subject of children.

Children are naturally very curious, and you may find that if you have children they'll begin to ask questions about your meditation practice. Try inviting them to join you, but don't force it. Our experience is that most children are open to learning about meditation, although (perhaps unsurprisingly) they rarely use it as an independent daily practice. The key thing is to inspire them by your practice. Don't hide it from them, and definitely avoid making them be quiet while you meditate. It's boring for everyone, and not only will they end up resenting your practice, you'll resent the inevitable noise they will make!

If they want to sit with you while you meditate, that's great. Encourage them to see how still they can be, or perhaps even count breaths together. We recommend only doing this for five or so minutes to start with, at the same time every day. Make it as much a part of your children's day as brushing their teeth or eating breakfast. If they are responsive, a short meditation together in the morning and before bed can assist in cognitive development and improve sleep.

Talk to your children about why you meditate, and explain that it helps you to be more fun and more creative. We have found that the more consistent our Integrated Meditation students are with their practice, the more their children encourage them to meditate, as they see the results in their parents.

top left *We think it's important not to force kids to meditate, but include them whenever they feel like it. Gentle suggestions can go far.*

top right *Instead of making your kids meditate, just be an excellent example of a meditator.*

bottom right *Two great teachers of mine: Maharishi Mahesh Yogi and my daughter, Marley. We have more to learn from kids than we can possibly teach them.*

Letting go

There is an ancient tale that I find helpful for considering the outcome versus the process:

A dedicated martial arts student went to his teacher and said earnestly, 'I am devoted to studying your system. How long will it take me to master it?'

The teacher's reply was very casual: 'Ten years,' he said.

The student was aghast, and impatiently answered, 'But I want to master it much faster than that. I will work very hard. I will practise every day, ten or more hours a day if I have to. How long will it take then?'

The teacher thought for a moment. 'Twenty years,' he said.

We're so used to seeing immediate results, and frequently even demand them. In Okinawan karate, the most ancient of all the karate lineages, the coloured belt system was only introduced after it became apparent that a simple white and black belt system was not hierarchical enough for Western students. Instead, a ladder-style system was needed to motivate trainees to keep progressing. This tells us a huge amount about the difference between Eastern and Western practices.

Keeping a beginner's mind is ideal for meditation. It really doesn't matter how long you have been practising. You must always stay curious, fresh and open to your practice – never stagnant or egotistical, thinking you have mastered something that cannot be mastered.

Meditation will provide your life with something initially intangible, and there's no overnight success story for the mind and consciousness. This can, at times, be frustrating in a world that constantly rewards concrete results. You may even find that those around you comment on the rewards of your daily meditation practice before you notice them yourself. Numerous students of The Broad Place say to their partners that they are considering stopping their practice, only to have their partners beg them not to, as the benefits are all too obvious. It's challenging for us to see ourselves objectively.

Developing mindfulness

There is a lot of discussion about mindfulness these days. We believe that mindfulness is meant to be the *output* of meditation, not a practice in itself.

You may come across concepts such as 'mindful colouring' and other activities that claim to be a part of a mindfulness practice. Though we believe these activities can be a wonderful way to unwind, they are best used alongside a regular meditation practice – otherwise it's like trying to get fit without exercising.

below *Spending time in nature is a beautiful way to return to our true nature. Meditation, journaling, drinking tea and exercise are all things we can try to do outside.*

High-Grade Living

Recognising true meditation

There are lots of meditative experiences that aren't necessarily meditation. Running, swimming and walking through a forest might be calming and relaxing, but they are *not* meditation. Meditation is a process whereby the mind does something very different to what it does all the time. The mind and body get to realign and rinse the body of stress, tension and fatigue. Some meditation techniques do this on a deep level, while other techniques simply take the body and mind out of fight-or-flight mode into a rest state. All are beneficial, but some are more transformative in the long term.

With the correct training and technique, absolutely anyone can meditate well. We know this from seeing so many people with no prior experience of meditation transform their lives.

Get very honest with yourself about what you are willing to commit to a practice, and then stretch beyond that a little. The mind that thinks it doesn't have time to meditate right now is the same mind that has not yet expanded enough to help you transform into a higher-grade you. Truly embrace the expression 'you don't know what you don't know'.

opposite *Sometimes it might feel like you can't see the forest for the trees with your meditation practice, and it's only when you step back and get a larger view that you start to see the impact it's having on your life. Remember to do this every six months to a year, and look at where you were compared to now, rather than focusing on each and every little meditation sitting and getting frustrated.*

Deepening your practice with a teacher

Part of your meditation journey is going to involve finding a teacher. Learning from a book or an app will never be as deep an experience as having a teacher with years upon years of experience to help you learn a technique and develop your practice. It's like learning to swim from the pages of a book versus with a teacher in the pool with you; it can be done, but having someone experienced, a master, helping you in real time will completely change your experience and your long-term technique.

Finding a teacher you like and trust will make your learning experience so much more wonderful. You need to find someone who has a distinct style that resonates with you so you can learn with relish and be inspired. I personally teach meditation because it has transformed my own life, and I continue to learn every year and share those learnings with students. I believe working with a teacher who is still immersed in study and daily practice is vital if you wish to continue to have an expansive practice yourself.

Like finding any health practitioner, it may take time and some trial and error. It's okay to move around. Try a number of different classes or workshops with different people and make notes on what worked for you. Did the teacher make you feel comfortable, inspired and at ease? Or did they make you feel unsure of yourself, like you were 'doing it wrong' or weren't cut out for meditation after all? True spirituality or self-development should never encourage you to lose your moral compass or be inauthentic. Finding teachers with integrity will help a lot with this. If you leave a class feeling like meditation 'isn't for you', then we guarantee it was the teacher who was the problem. Meditation is for everybody.

Working with a meditation teacher should be a creative experience that inspires you to be disciplined in your practice and, ultimately, realistic about your progress. I am fortunate to have studied under many teachers, some who have taught me powerful and rich lessons filled with integrity, and others who have taught me powerful lessons on what I don't wish to be as a teacher myself. In truth, a teacher can only show you the path, sharing knowledge

opposite *The idea is to be as clear and transparent as you can be with yourself, and your teacher.*

following pages *Every single student, and every single human being, is different and unique, and should be cherished as such. Don't try to fit in or water down yourself or your practice – celebrate your unique experience as a human, and as a meditator.*

for a student to understand in their own way. There is a wonderful Zen story about a student who asked a senior monk, 'How do I find enlightenment?' The teacher smiled and said, 'Look here', pointing to the moon, which represents something bigger than the mind can comprehend – nature, the universe, totality. However, the student looked at the teacher's finger and then followed it down their arm, finishing on the teacher, and concluded that the teacher was the path to enlightenment. They mistook the finger for the moon. It's a common mistake, but the teacher is simply a guide. As a teacher, I hope my students never mistake me for the moon. Instead, I hope I can burn bright and light a path for students, whatever route they may take.

High-Grade Living

Understanding the experience

As one ancient Zen story goes, a student went to his meditation teacher and said, 'My meditation is horrible! I feel so distracted, or my legs ache, or I'm constantly falling asleep. It's just horrible!'

'It will pass,' the teacher said matter-of-factly.

A week later, the student came back to his teacher. 'My meditation is wonderful! I feel so aware, so peaceful, so alive! It's just wonderful!'

'It will pass,' the teacher replied matter-of-factly.

We can frequently get attached to a 'good' experience in meditation, and then get frustrated when we can't achieve that experience again. We can try to figure out why, but there's rarely a clear answer. Part of a meditation practice is working with the mystery and continuing to get in the chair no matter what the last sitting was like. It all evens out over time.

There is a Japanese concept known as *mushotoku*, which means acting without interest in personal gain and giving without expecting anything in return. Simply being present is all that's required. It certainly goes against the prevailing modern Western thought, which fixates on constant acquisition and gain. The idea that we can give without needing a reward is one of the key principles of Zen and can really challenge a Western mind.

Mushotoku breeds freedom and happiness; you cannot lose what you have gained because there is nothing to lose or gain. The *mushotoku* mindset removes the anxiety that comes with want and replaces it with peace. It is important to note that *mushotoku* is not about removing yourself from the world. It is about lack of attachment on a mental level and is a very sincere practice that enhances meditation.

Embracing ritual

Ritual is not necessary as part of a modern meditation practice, but it can be a beautiful and valuable addition. Finding quiet in your heart through ritual is a wonderful way to stay centred. In Eastern traditions, ritual punctuated many components of the day, particularly meditation and spiritual practices. You may not be able to go back to a simpler time from centuries or decades ago, but you can regain a sense of pause and wholeness by incorporating a few simple rituals into your daily life.

right *You can look to many lineages of meditation and spirituality for inspiration with ritual. The Hindu god Ganesh is a favourite of mine: representing strength, wisdom and patience, he is called upon as the remover of blocks in life. I call on him quite a lot for strength in my life.*

Working with scent

The beauty of incense is that its scent shifts slowly and eventually dissipates, allowing for a more detailed sensory experience. The smell and sound of a match lighting, the sight of the incense catching the flame and the smoke wafting about in the early morning light, can be very grounding.

When choosing incense, make sure to find a scent that resonates with you and, if possible, stick to ones made with natural materials.

We recommend finding a lovely holder for your incense sticks rather than just putting them in any available container. Japanese-style holders made from copper and brass look beautiful in their minimalist aesthetic. Use matches rather than a lighter to make the ceremony of lighting the incense feel more traditional and special.

Working with candles

In Japan, legend has it that candles came with the spread of Buddhism during the Nara period in the eighth century. Candles were a way to connect to an ancestral line, a part of meditation, and used in visits to temples and other ceremonies. In India, lighting a candle plays an important role in Vedic ceremonies, inviting in warmth and recognition, and honouring those who have stood before us sharing wisdom.

Simply lighting a candle before your meditation can be a beautiful way to ritualise your practice. Source natural, handmade Japanese candles and iron holders for a beautiful set-up, or use natural beeswax candles. It's a good idea to avoid scented candles if you're already using incense in your practice.

right *An altar can be as small as a single crystal, candle and wee statue, such as Ganesh here. We have so many Ganesh statues in our home.*

Finding stillness in tea

Incorporating a Taoist tea ceremony, or *chadō*, into your morning practice is a wonderful way to begin your day, warming your body and mind.

Taoism is a philosophy native to China and focuses on aligning oneself with nature and one's own truth. There is a principle in *chadō*, 'Never pick up the kettle until you have stilled your heart', that is useful to apply to all aspects of your day.

The key to a beautiful tea ritual is in the details. For some, that will mean sourcing the best quality teas, high-grade spring water and handmade ceramics that you absolutely adore. It's also about noticing the little things, from the warmth of the cup and the rising steam to the textures and flavours involved. It's a journey of meditation unto itself when done with complete presence.

Ultimately there is no one formula for a tea ceremony any more than there is a formula for life. There are particular tea sequences you can learn, but the most important thing is being present in the moment and the details.

right *I practise a traditional tea ceremony from a Zen lineage, and sitting with friends to share tea is one of my favourite things to do. Within the Zen lineage, tea ceremonies are called* chadō, *which is the art of presence, harmony and healing.*

High-Grade Living

Creating an altar

An altar doesn't necessarily need to have religious connotations. It's simply a spiritual space that can be aesthetically delightful and uniquely you.

Consider what's important to you and find items that connect with this. They might be aligned to your religion or a philosophy you believe in, or you could use a photograph of a loved one or a beloved teacher. You might introduce some nature with a little vase and a single flower. Your altar can be as detailed or as simple as you like.

If you're concerned about space, or have children or animals who may think that your altar is an exciting new game, it certainly doesn't mean you have to miss out. Think outside the box – or in this case, in the box – by tucking your altar away in a cupboard or a drawer that you can open when it's time to enjoy it.

An altar can be used in any way you like. You may wish to meditate in front of it, or simply bow your head to it each morning and night. How you interact with it is up to you.

High-Grade Living

Incorporating prayer

You don't have to be religious to invite prayer into your life. Sitting with your eyes closed and speaking quietly with the universe, nature and yourself is a very moving experience.

Examples include:

Dear universe, thank you for your support. Please guide me today with integrity. Please help remove blocks from my path and allow the day to flow with grace.

Dear spirit, please help me align completely with my true self and not be swayed by all the 'shoulds' or by my overthinking mind.

One well-known prayer is the serenity prayer:

God, grant me the serenity to accept the things I cannot change, the courage to change the things I can, and the wisdom to know the difference.

You don't have to use any of these examples. Instead, try writing your own.

opposite A tiny hole-in-the-wall altar I saw in North India while studying and travelling there.

below *We have peppered throughout our home these little totems to remind us of our natural state, which should be grounded, centred and calm. The concepts of being held and being multi-faceted are ideas we return to often.*

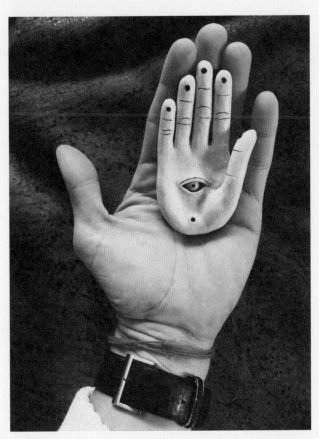

Expanding the mind

A brief period of reading helps expand the mind after meditation. Once the mind is stilled and calmed, information goes in at a deeper level. A book that you dive into each day after meditating, such as the *Tao Te Ching* (we like Stephen Mitchell's translation) or *Meditations* by Marcus Aurelius, can be a wonderful way to absorb a small amount of information with high impact.

opposite *A mobile tea ceremony kit that I like to travel with and a copy of* Meditations *by Marcus Aurelius, one of my daily reads.*

top *Meditating with a friend and creating a coherent energy between the two of you is a powerful practice.*

bottom *Meditating while travelling can be tricky. We love staying in apartments, as they usually have a lounge area where we can do yoga and meditate with more space. Especially if one of us is tired, the other can go into another space for their practice and not disturb the one resting.*

Seeing the big picture

The key to any meditation practice is discipline. You simply won't experience anything new if you don't apply yourself. We like to teach students that meditating twice a day for twenty minutes accounts for 3 per cent of their day. We meditate to enhance the other 97 per cent.

Remember to approach your practice with patience and a willingness to learn, but also give yourself a break if you don't feel like you're connecting with it just yet. Let go of excuses and the idea that you're not doing it enough or not doing it right. You'll find that you'll see results much sooner this way.

You can never master meditation. We meditate to master life, not the other way around. Meditation is about discipline, consistency and dedication, and there are no shortcuts to a truly committed meditation practice.

right *Meditating at a temple in Japan.*

High-Grade Living

Diving into Meditation

Your Home as a Retreat

A home is a retreat from our hyper-engaged modern lives, a place to renew and nourish ourselves. It is a canvas where we can audit, edit and refine the direction we wish our lives to follow. A beautifully curated home is one that speaks authentically to us about the high-grade life we want to live. It has its foundations in where and how we live, and its roots in how we eat, and nourish our minds and bodies.

Creating your high-grade home is an ongoing, individual process that will be unique to you. For some, it will mean absolute minimalism, paring back to the bare essentials. For others, it means developing a collection of personal and meaningful art, books and objects.

Think of this chapter as a journey through your home, but with a deep sense of purpose and alignment with who you are and your values. This process is about creating an intentional and customised home environment that brings you joy. A luxurious home does not have to mean expensive furniture and famous art. The new luxury is about meaning and delight, and provides you with a platform for experience and growth.

left *An owl would hoot all through the night in the huge gum tree outside the window, keeping us company as we all slept in close quarters in our tiny cottage in Palm Beach, Sydney, Australia.*

opposite, top left *Our rescue dog Honey reminds us of the importance of retreating and staying cosied up.*

opposite, top right *Our visiting cockatoos at Palm Beach remind us to have a laugh.*

opposite, bottom left *Immersing ourselves in nature constantly, with yoga, karate, study, dining and reading all taking place outside, changed our wellbeing and connection to nature and each other immensely.*

opposite, bottom right *The fairy-tale backyard of the pink house backed onto a nature reserve, which helped us return to ourselves.*

High-Grade Living

Turning life upside down

Arran and I tried an experiment in early 2016. We wanted to find out whether we owned our things, or they possessed us. We had been discussing this idea for years and years: what if we, as adults, re-created our home from the ground up? What could we learn?

We had spent the summer house-sitting for friends on their stunning 60-acre property in Byron Bay. The house was only half finished, so there were very few appliances and only a handful of bowls and cutlery. We washed the dishes after every meal and spent our days barefoot at the beach, on the river and cooking and eating outside. Marley was too scared to sleep downstairs on her own, so she slept on a mattress in our room with our dog Honey, and we essentially camped our way through this time. The simplicity of our days together, in constant orbit and flow, was life-changing. Immersed in sun and sea, we were able to rebuild on every level.

I had to return to Sydney a week early, and I will never forget walking into our huge, glass, designer-filled rental home and feeling nauseated. The place suddenly felt hollow, and I ached for nature and Arran and Marley like a fever. I wandered around opening windows and doors to let in fresh air, but it didn't matter how much poured in; I felt like I couldn't breathe. I realised that we couldn't live like this any longer – financially, physically and emotionally stretched as individuals and as a family.

I started to look up beachside rentals in Palm Beach, where I grew up and my parents still lived. I found a fully furnished cottage, set on the exact nature reserve where I used to play as a child. The rent was almost half of what we were currently paying, and once I saw it I could see why: it was also a quarter of the size. However, it was stunning beyond belief – adorable and retro, with a light-filled garden and glimpses of the ocean from the front and back.

We committed to the experiment and gave away or sold almost all of our possessions, donating the proceeds to charity. The ancient philosopher Atticus once said, 'What a strange world. We trade our days for things.' This rang a little too true for us back then. We had invested a lot of time and energy into buying and acquiring objects, and we felt we needed to

opposite The beautiful property of our friends Kim and Stephen, whose home we cared for whilst they were away, and whose dog, Chief, became our pup-nephew for life. This is where we would sit, build fires, cook, paddle down the river, and while away hours upon hours over that special summer.

following pages, right *A return home: Palm Beach in Sydney, Australia, was where I grew up and then resettled after having my daughter, only to fly off again and eventually come back for a large chapter that reshaped our lives forever.*

change. I had thought this would be a beautiful experience, at once both cathartic and charitable. In truth, it was gruelling, sweaty and devastatingly disappointing. No one wanted our things, even though we had paid a fortune for them. They were basically worthless to everyone else. There was a glut of items in second-hand stores, and charities were reluctant to take our donations due to lack of space. It was a giant lesson for us in consumerism.

I also thought owning very little would be a liberating experience, and in some ways I was right, but at times it was also scary. I would wake up in the middle of the night in a sweat and find myself counting all the things I no longer had: a fridge, washing machine, blender, iron...things I felt I should own at this stage of my life. We were all so close that I would lie in bed listening to everyone, even the dog, breathing from the other room.

Yet as I was getting accustomed to living without a dishwasher, I discovered other things, like how wonderful it was to wash the dishes in the tiny sink while looking out the window into the beautiful garden, filled with sandstone paths and frangipani trees, and a mishmash of Australian botanicals and European shrubs. I grew so fond of glancing up while cooking dinner to see Arran walking up the path to come home. In the morning, the sun tinged the pale-blue kitchen pink, and the steam from the kettle danced in the light.

Without all the distractions that a huge home has to offer, we instead spent most of our time outdoors: lying in the garden, walking through the nature reserve, swimming in the ocean. Spending so much more time together as a family than we ever had before. It would be a lie to say that I found myself completely letting go of material things, but during this time I learned to let go of them when I needed to and enjoy just simply being with my loved ones.

right *The sun streamed into the pink house in Palm Beach, Sydney, Australia, through the kitchen in the morning and through the backyard in the evening. Every morning we stretched, made coffee, chatted with the myriad birds and rested before launching into our days. I would put all our crystals out to rest during the full moon, and when the night was empty of clouds, the light was so bright we could barely sleep. Honey and our daughter, Marley, shared a bunk bed, the dog on the bottom, and I would creep in during a full moon to watch them both breathe deeply in their sleep late in the evening.*

High-Grade Living

Understanding your patterns

Take time to really think about what is important to you and
what has been driving your purchases, then respond to these
questions in your journal:

- What ultimately brings you happiness?
- What gives you contentment?
- How easy is it for you to embrace simplicity
  over complexity?
- What do your purchases reveal about you?
- How does this inform you moving forward?

Say goodbye to home myths

Whenever we elevate a certain part of our lives, we may have to let go of some outdated thinking. Some lingering myths around creative homes include:

- it has to be a designer brand to be excellent design
- good design is expensive
- you can't mix and match old and new
- you have to have design qualifications to create a space
- you should bring in experts to manage the whole process of designing or styling your home
- experts have incredible homes themselves (the truth is that they often don't have the time to work on them!)
- design and styling are feminine interests and professions

The truth is that personal style isn't something that can be taught, nor should it be. A high-grade home is a place where you can be your most authentic self, and who better to create that space than you? You can certainly look to professional opinions and knowledge for guidance, but anyone on any budget can design a space and a sanctuary for themselves. This chapter will guide you through creating your authentic home.

opposite *Our rescue dog Honey, greeting the morning sun.*

right *Kim Amos, our friend who owns River Hawk Ranch in Byron Bay, Australia, has always embraced mixing old with new, unconventionally painting walls charcoal and pinning to those walls items collected on travels. It's like the walls breathe with stories.*

Expressing creatively

The audit, edit and refine principle is best employed to understand your creative expression. Most of the time we need to clear out before we can invite in. It's very hard to get a clear view of where you can enhance and flourish in and among chaos. So dive deeply and then invite in your creative expression. Answering the following questions should help.

- When you view your home, and its uses and purposes, how are you creatively expressing yourself?
- Can areas of your home potentially become less fixed and more fluid?
- Does the art reflect you and your creativity?
- Does the furniture feel like an accurate expression of who you are?
- Creativity is light, fun, dynamic. Does your home reflect this?
- How could you create more space for creative expression within each room?

opposite *The windows of the tree house in Palm Beach, Sydney, Australia, reminded us of Japanese houses, rickety, beautiful, worn. We kept the rooms themselves minimal to focus on these. This room morphed continually as a tea ceremony room, meditation mentoring room, reading room, and also as a family movie room – the only room with a small TV nestled on a tree stump we had sawn down from our firewood.*

Sharing your spaces

With fresh eyes, look at each room in your house and how it is used, and then respond to the following in your journal:

- How can you enhance the use of this space?
- Should some things be moved to different spaces?
- How can you create an area for ritual in your home?
- Is there a space that could become a dedicated reading nook? Or a place to draw and be creative?

High-Grade Living

Living with peace

There is an ancient Zen story that we can all keep in mind when thinking about how we live:

There was once a person who was considering relocating to a new village. He approached the Zen master who lived there and asked, 'Do you think I will like this village? Are the people nice?'

'What are the people like in the village where you come from?' the Zen master replied.

'Well, they are nasty and greedy. They are angry and live for cheating and stealing,' said the newcomer.

'Those are exactly the types of people we have in this village,' replied the master.

Later, another newcomer to the village visited the Zen master and asked the same question. The master replied again, 'What are the people like in the village where you come from?'

'They are sweet and live in harmony. They care for one another and for the land. They respect each other and are seekers of spirit,' said the newcomer.

'Those are exactly the types of people we have in this village,' said the master.

Your attitude determines your life experience. You create your reality from your own perspective. At some point, you will probably think there is somewhere better you could be living – a more interesting location, a nicer house with a prettier garden. However, working with what you have in this moment is the essence of high-grade living. Pining for an imaginary future strips you of joy for the now.

Empty out

The Japanese concept of *kyo-jitsu* explains that when something is too full, something else has to empty. It's a term frequently used in energetics (*ki*), macrobiotics and health.

In the Western world, it's common for us to just concentrate on filling, acquiring more of this, more of that. Even spiritually, there is a push to become 'more fulfilled'. This attitude comes at a cost, as it can create a drain on something else.

The key is balance, and this applies to design too. Some wonderful examples can be found in temples and their use of negative space. One area might be very detailed and full, and an opposing area spacious and serene.

Balance doesn't mean you must even out all aspects of your life so you're putting the same amount of energy into everything, and this applies to your home as well. It's more about carving out a little more here, and filling a touch more there, sometimes on a dramatic scale. Where can you live at a fast pace, and where can you slow down? Where can you create space and breadth, and where can you overflow a little? What can you absorb, and what can you resist?

right This corner of the Palm Beach tree house in Sydney, Australia, we would move around constantly, working new plants into the sunlight that the afternoon gifted them, and adding furniture for entertaining or for hosting teachers, large meditation events and dinner parties. We are never afraid of moving things around so the house breathes life and is never stagnant.

top *Being set on a sprawling national park meant we had tonnes of overgrown trees and plants in our garden; we would collect stalks that fell in storms and bring them inside the house.*

bottom *The same corner as before, with plants and fallen palm fronds that we would hang to dry out; they appear as coral on the floor.*

High-Grade Living

Understanding *zanshin*

Zanshin is a Zen term that means appreciating the entire cosmos at all times. It is a state of utter present awareness of everything that is, where the mind is completely at peace and observant of all things. It is the recognition that everything is connected and that the entire universe is based on our perceptions and our projections of reality.

When you observe simply what is, you can see the beauty in the entire sequence of events, or nature, of your life. *Zanshin* is about appreciating with complete presence that everything is important – walking, dressing, sitting in traffic, drinking a coffee. It avoids favouring certain activities and embraces every act with reverence.

Zanshin can pull you away from materialism and into appreciation. It's less about the objects you have around you, and more about the energy and the atmosphere you create, and the love that can be shared within your home.

Keeping a clean home

Most people tend to feel calmer in a tidy space. Zen temples and minimalist interiors usually feel soothing and relaxing, with symmetry creating a sense of order not just in the room, but in our minds. Shoukei Matsumoto, a Buddhist monk, describes the home as being a reflection of the heart: clean home, clean heart. Remember this and you may find you clean your home not out of a sense of duty, but as a practice to keep your heart clean as well. Somehow it makes the whole process far more enjoyable!

Inviting nature into your home

You might not have a beautiful garden, but bringing nature inside adds such aliveness to each space. Taking care of indoor plants requires work, but it improves the air quality and adds a sense of serenity.

Go through each room in your home and see what you could add to bring nature inside. If you don't feel confident with plants, you can always use branches or twigs – anything to bring nature into each space.

High-Grade Living

opposite and above *Just as nature is never perfect, bringing nature into your home also doesn't have to mean a perfect bunch of flowers. It can be plants, cacti, twigs, branches and more.*

Taking time for yourself

Often, and especially when you live with others, seeking out time for yourself usually means getting out of the house. We create these beautiful spaces to cultivate presence and creativity, and leave them in search of those very things!

It's so important to schedule home-alone time for everyone living in your home. Getting everyone else out of the house and just relaxing and pottering about may seem indulgent at first, but it's essential when living in a shared environment.

Time for yourself can certainly take some planning if you are sharing spaces with flatmates or young children. However, the kindness and compassion that flows from us when we have had time to retreat in our own environment can only contribute to a happy home.

Yohaku

The blank space within Japanese art is called *yohaku*. Surrounding the painted parts with space celebrates and enhances them. This is a concept you can invite into your life as well: the spaces around your activities can heighten your experiences. When everything is rushed or scheduled too tightly, there is no *yohaku*. Ultimately, this leaves us feeling exhausted.

Cultivating *yohaku* in your life could include finding space to sit and breathe deeply between meetings, slowing down your heart rate and mind. Try starting the morning without technology, giving yourself space before the day's activities and noise begin. And when at work, take regular breaks by moving away from your desk or your current task to re-centre.

Mindful eating

Eating constitutes such a large part of our health, both mental and physical. We nourish our bodies through what we eat, and much of our health is directed by our gut and what we consume. But we don't give this much credit or thought when we are rushing about, barely present. Here are some things to consider.

High-grade eating, or mindful eating, is simply paying attention to what you are doing. This is critically important for physical and emotional health. Ask yourself why you are eating. So often we use food for comfort. We eat because we are angry, lonely, stressed and tired. Recognise the reason for eating, and the enjoyment and benefit it provides. Work out what foods make you feel grounded and what foods make you feel anxious. Does eating make you feel sleepy or energised?

When you eat with intention to nourish your body – when all your awareness is aligned with nourishment, and you chew and swallow with presence – your body can digest the food much more easily. You aren't what you eat; you are what you digest. Slow down and be present for all of it.

Preparing food with meaning

How we prepare our food informs the experience of the person eating it. At Zen monasteries in Japan, the *tenzo* is the head chef, and the mindset of this person is incredibly important. A calm mind results in calm food.

In India, the birthplace of Ayurveda, avoiding cooking when angry and creating nourishing environments in which to prepare food is seen as just as necessary as having a pot and a stove at hand.

One of the most wonderful things about eating in countries such as Italy and Spain is the simplicity. A few ingredients of the best quality – one or two tomatoes, some basil and a ball of buffalo mozzarella, or a soft peach, a hunk of goat's cheese and a piece of freshly baked baguette – make the most magical meals. When you are working with excellent ingredients, there's no need to trick things up. So source better quality and serve it simply.

top and bottom *We have eaten in so many exquisite restaurants around the world, but nothing beats a home-cooked meal from the heart. Our favourite meals have always involved standing in a kitchen with friends, cooking, sipping drinks, playing music and chatting away before settling in for a long meal. One cold winter in Osaka, Japan, Tok Kise and Hiromi Karatsu, the founders of Truck Furniture, cooked us a traditional meal, teaching me every part of the process while Arran chose records to play and the dogs ran amok.*

following pages *Any meal, even a humble croissant or crumpet, can be made special with beautiful dishware, quality honey, jams and salted butter. Eat seated somewhere lovely, and you have yourself a high-grade meal.*

Eating with meaning

When eating, simply eat. Don't watch television or scan the newspaper or read a book. Be completely present for the experience of eating – the scents, the flavours, the textures. Absorb them all. With each mouthful, chew slowly. Feel the food in your mouth and how the texture changes with each bite. Ensure each mouthful is ready for your digestion.

Take the time to consider what's on your plate – the time it took to grow, to source, and to make its way to you. Is it a deep-sea fish? Where was it caught? What kind of water does it live in? How long did that vegetable take to grow? Was it above ground, deep in the soil or on a tree? What country and region did it grow in? This thoughtfulness creates an incredible reverence and sense of awe and gratitude for each meal.

High-Grade Living

Presence and prayer

Here are two simple Buddhist prayers you can say before meals, either out loud or internally.

Shokuzen

Many lives and much hard work have gone into the blessing that is this meal. I will show my appreciation by enjoying this food with a deep sense of gratitude.

Shokugo

I thank you for the wonderful meal, with deep gratitude, respect and reverence.

Your Home as a Retreat

Audit, edit and refine

Our homes are our sanctuaries and should serve as inviting retreats from the frenzy of the exterior world. Ask yourself, how does your home feel when you walk into it? What ambience does it offer? Is it comfortable and inviting, or is it a mess? To improve the impact your home has on your daily life, begin with an audit, edit and refine.

First is the audit, where you assess your surroundings. As you audit each room in your home, keep in mind the following questions:

- What is triggering a materialistic response?
- Are you consuming or hoarding to mask anything?
- Are you culling too violently or controlling too much?
- Which rooms are inviting and provide calm and tranquillity?
- Which rooms feel hectic?
- What kind of home do you want to have?
- Some people are very frugal by nature, and prefer practicality over beauty. Is this your preferred way of living?
- Some people are very extravagant and showy, and prefer beauty over practicality. Is this your preferred way of living?

Remember, there is no right or wrong kind of home. This is the beauty of high-grade living – you get to create the home you actually want that allows your best self to shine through. This process is about releasing yourself from all the 'shoulds' in your home, moving toward an intuitive way of living, and having your home support you through that. Understanding more deeply your own sense of beauty, what you desire and love, as opposed to the current trends in magazines and on blogs, is a process that will take curiosity and openness. This is the essence of high-grade living.

After auditing, the process of editing begins. This isn't about giving away everything you own! However, a giant culling of all your objects is worthwhile in the reframing of what a high-grade home means to you.

Ask yourself what has meaning and what has simply accumulated over the years. If there's an item in your home

opposite, top left *Our pink house in Palm Beach, Sydney, Australia, which was the catalyst for us to give away and sell almost everything we owned.*

opposite, top right *Our motley crew of plates – a mix of antiques, market finds and handmade – that comes together as quite the collection, each with a story.*

opposite, bottom *For me, this picture is the essence of our home life: beautiful and a little bit chaotic, surrounded by things that were made for us by our friends and collected on travels. We had this table custom-made from an old door, and we all sit on the floor to eat, a habit we adopted in Japan. We combined the lounge room with the dining room so it could be the centre of the home at all times. Meals are informal, but can be long, languid and filled with conversation and shared moments. Around this very table we have had lunches for fourteen friends that turned into dinners, events with students, lessons from visiting teachers who stayed with us, and birthday parties for our daughter. We feel the dining table is the heart of the home.*

High-Grade Living

that's broken or doesn't have meaning or purpose, donate it and move it on.

What begins to occur through the editing process is that you start to recognise certain habits and patterns. Your potentially irrelevant and redundant ways of living start to become evident. It's incredibly cathartic. You will begin to see how you hold onto things in various areas of your life and where you could be letting go more frequently.

You may find you're attached to certain things simply because they're extravagant or expensive, but they don't bring any real value to your home or your life. These purchases are often made on a whim, or during times when you've felt stressed and uncertain and needed some retail therapy. It's important to be honest!

Next, you refine. Refining is the process of gently revisiting a particular area to help it upgrade along with yourself and your life as you grow and evolve. It helps avoid stagnancy and aids you in engaging with areas of your life instead of getting stuck, or having life fly by you. If you avoid refining, then you will end up back where you started. Refining doesn't need to be laborious; it should instead be embraced as a mindful philosophy. Look around your home and ask yourself these questions:

- Is this reflective of who I am and how I want to live?
- Does my home now support me (and/or those I live with) in ways that are nourishing?

Revisiting this process once a year will help your home evolve and not become stagnant. If we didn't acquire a single new item, and didn't change as people, this wouldn't be necessary. However, we are constantly evolving, and our spaces of retreat must come along for the ride. Deliberate choices create a curated life rather than a chaotic one.

opposite *Having always lived in rentals, we use the floor a lot to display art and things we love – the benefit being that you have continued flexibility and can move things around as much as you like, so spaces become free-flowing and not stuck or stagnant. In Arran's design and art studio that was at the bottom of our garden, we painted the floor white and used it as a showcase for art and objects.*

following pages *Our work and home life have always blurred, and The Broad Place students become like extended family. We have them into our home for meals, picnics and shared experiences as well as courses and education. It may not be conventional, but the normal barriers are immediately lifted when you have someone in your home, and for us, a space to learn and grow means feeling comfortable and 'at home'.*

High-Grade Living

High-grade wardrobe

How much decision-making power is taken up by choosing what to wear in the morning? Do you spend ages sifting through piles of clothes that don't quite fit, need ironing or don't work together? Imagine spending that time meditating instead and what a difference that could make to your day.

Auditing your wardrobe

Take some time to look through your wardrobe and journal your first impressions, considering the following:

- Is your wardrobe representative of how you want to live?

- Is it creative and dynamic, with bold styles that change daily? Or is it a minimal wardrobe with structure and quality that helps you dress rapidly without much brainpower required?

- Are there clothes that don't fit or are uncomfortable?

- Is there anything that needs mending and can be saved?

- Is there anything outdated that is simply taking up space?

Editing your wardrobe

Have a look at your audit and see what jumps out at you. Anything that no longer fits or is uncomfortable to wear has to go. High-grade living is about feeling as good and as comfortable with yourself as you can.

Go through all the items you feel might need to move on, and consider the following questions:

- Can it be donated to charity? If so, do it. We should all donate generously and consciously. But be aware that many

charities don't take clothing that is damaged. Too often charity organisations spend valuable time sorting through donations that people simply can't wear.

- If anything is damaged beyond repair, can it be recycled? Many damaged clothes can be cut into rags and cloths for cleaning. And any colourful or patterned items can be cut up to use as gorgeous and sustainable wrapping for a gift.

- Is there any way the clothing you want to keep can be stored more carefully so it lasts longer?

Refining your wardrobe

Now that your wardrobe has been cleansed, consider what you have learned. Let this inform your future buying.

Avoid buying things for 'special occasions' if you can, as the cost per wear is usually very high. Consider instead renting an outfit, which is both cheaper and more sustainable. There are some fantastic stores both on the high street and online that have a huge range of designer labels you can rent for a steal.

Keep refining your wardrobe as you go through different moods and stages in your personal style. Keeping it fluid keeps it creative.

top *Moving from a four-bedroom home into a tiny two-bedroom cottage meant 80 per cent of our clothes had to go, and the rest had to fit into this single wardrobe. We both learnt so much about our beliefs around how many clothes we thought we needed. For years Arran and I limited our wardrobe palette to white, grey and navy for simplicity. Years on, Arran still sticks to this.*

bottom *Even Honey has a little wardrobe for winter.*

High-Grade Living

High-grade kitchen

A kitchen cleanse can be one of the most satisfying edits of the house. It will hold all kinds of insights into how you are living and eating. Your kitchen is the heart of nourishment for you and your family and friends. Over the years, my family has had incredible kitchens: open plan, with plenty of storage and amazing appliances. We've also had the most hobbit-hole-of-hell kitchens, with no storage and cockroaches flying out of the itty-bitty cupboards. And I have always tried to make them work, giving myself over to the lessons that each kitchen taught me.

I have to admit that the same beautiful food has come from each and every kitchen, because it's the heart that goes into the dish that matters, not the kitchen it was made in. So begin to view your kitchen as a little temple to your heart and see how that can flow into your food. If you have ever been camping, you will know that simple food cooked with presence tastes amazing, even with just one cooker and one pan!

Auditing your kitchen

Take a really good look around your kitchen. Look in the cupboards and all the drawers, and don't forget the fridge. Journal your responses to these questions:

- What do you see, organisation or chaos?
- Are there any ingredients you can't remember buying?
- Is there an exotic and intriguing group of ingredients?
- Are your essentials neatly displayed?
- Are there fundamental staples you can't live without?
- Can you barely see these through a sea of products and ingredients?

Editing your kitchen

If you are hanging onto food you don't use, the edit will be insightful – and possibly painful. The many cooking shows and books out there are great for inspiration, but the downside is that a lot of us enthusiastically purchase things we use just a pinch from once. If you find yourself asking, 'What did I even buy that for?', it can go. Being very honest is important. Having a pantry filled with fantasy items doesn't inspire us to cook each day; it just makes us feel guilty and ashamed.

The kitchen edit involves not just food, but appliances, crockery, utensils – everything! Here are some things to consider as you edit:

- Is any food out of date? Throwing away what seems like perfectly good food can be confronting, but it will help reprogram how you buy food in the future.

- Are there any items that you don't use? This includes things like the fancy spices you bought on a whim, or those four different jars of pink Himalayan salt. Consolidate what you can, and move everything else on. Then once you think you have finished, do it again. You will be much better at this the second time around.

- Are there any crockery or utensil items that have been sitting at the bottom of the cupboard for months or years? Donate them! The same goes for that fancy appliance you've only used once since being gifted it at Christmas.

Refining your kitchen

Fill your kitchen with only the very best ceramics, cookware and ingredients, and keep it really simple. Less is more in the kitchen. It's not going to happen overnight; it will take time, heart and patience. Enjoy where the process takes you.

USE YOUR BEST EVERY DAY

Are the items you love most not being used very often because they are 'precious'? High-grade living is not about saving things up for a special day. It's about using your best quality every day. Use your best glasses at every meal. Your favourite plates are perfect for toast and tea on a rainy day. Try to mix it up, not favouring a single type of bowl but experimenting with different types. We shop a lot for handmade ceramics and always for vintage, so every single plate and cup is different. Try mixing it up to make every meal more creative, instead of having eight matching white plates!

opposite Grower's markets are an amazing opportunity to source ingredients and recipes from local growers. This is a chard and goat cheese tart that a vegetable grower suggested I make, and he was right – the combination was delicious.

above The utterly impressive and beautiful collection of plates from Hiromi Karatsu, who can explain where every single one came from!

top left *Cooking over a fire takes you outdoors and can be an interactive way to prepare meals.*

top right *Eating outdoors also holds a special place in our hearts, and somehow you always seem to fit in more food when eating outside. Here we had a very long lunch with our friends in Los Angeles, USA, where everyone brought many things that we prepared together.*

bottom left *When we lived in Palm Beach, Sydney, Australia, we barely wore shoes and ate most of our meals outdoors, even in winter.*

opposite *We have always had a large community of friends who are also into food and sharing things they make – like our neighbour Virginia, who used to gift us her special handmade chili oil that we would use on top of everything!*

High-grade bathroom

There is a lot to audit, edit and refine in a bathroom: medicines, make-up, beauty samples, towels with stains, half-empty shampoos, a weird toothbrush that doesn't seem to belong to anybody...the list goes on. A bathroom audit, edit and refine may not seem as much fun as tackling a wardrobe; however, we promise the results are worth it.

Auditing your bathroom

Imagine the type of high-grade life you can have if you adopt:

- simplified morning routines
- luxurious bathing rituals
- a minimal and clean aesthetic to match your bathing and beauty routines

If you want to say yes to even one of the above, you need to start your bathroom audit, edit and refine immediately. It will take less time than you think. Look around your bathroom and journal your responses to these questions:

- What are your beauty routine essentials?
- Are the items displayed neatly, or is the space cluttered and disorganised?
- Are there any products you don't use anymore or that are past their use-by date?
- Do you have any repeat products that you can combine into a single item? For example, multiple hair products that do the same thing.

Editing your bathroom

First of all, grab yourself a bin, because it's unlikely you will find someone who wants your half-used bits and pieces. Anything that hasn't been touched in 3–6 months has to go.

Consider the following as you clear out those drawers and cupboards:

- What are you holding onto that isn't needed? What can you remove?
- What can be passed on to someone else? If you know of any teenagers who would absolutely love your half-used expensive lipstick that you decided didn't suit you, by all means give it away. Just remember to sterilise first.
- How many products and appliances do you actually need for bathing, hair care, cosmetic routines, etc.?

Eliminate clutter with presence and care. Avoid a negative attitude and stay focused and positive about the impact these actions will have. Sometimes when removing items, we can get caught up in negative thinking about our wastefulness to date, and this is an important part of recognising our previous actions. Acknowledgement helps us rewire our brains so that we avoid the same behaviour in the future.

opposite *Don't be afraid to incorporate items you might not normally think would work in a bathroom. Objects, art and plants all work beautifully and can really elevate the space.*

Refining your bathroom

Begin to think of your bathroom as another sanctuary, and treat it as such. Maybe over time you'll realise you want more plants (they thrive in bathrooms) or colour in there. Keep reducing the number of products you purchase. I always find travel interesting, as it gives me insight into what products I am actually using and what I am just hoarding – since only so much can come with me. Keep an eye on what you spend your money on and what comes into the house. With all the amazing products on the market, the bathroom can become either a beautiful resource for self-care, or an overflowing mountain of expensive things you simply do not need.

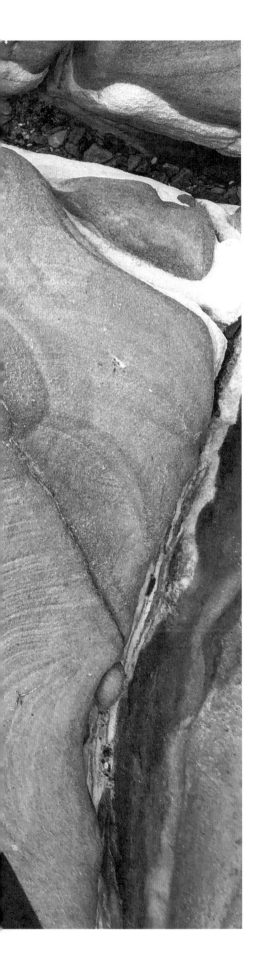

Expanding Your Creativity

High-Grade Living

Creativity is a life pursuit. It informs how we relate, converse, dress, prepare our food, work, make a home, travel and live on every level. It extends well beyond painting, sculpting and making music; creativity is actually about living in an expansive way, being curious and exploring new frontiers. We truly believe that every single person has the capacity to be creative.

Creativity can expand every task into something more enjoyable. Every time we navigate away from a challenge and into a solution, we are using our creativity. We have found that if you *do* have experience in artistic areas, and are used to coming up with colour pairings, putting shapes together, sculpting, making, using the hands and mind together, then those experiences can certainly assist in bringing about a creative approach in all areas of life. If you have no experience with artistic pursuits, don't worry. This chapter is all about helping you start this free-flowing formation of ideas.

left *Our dear friend Jeff Kober, who embodies the creative process as an actor, photographer and meditation teacher, always curious, documenting, listening and keeping his eyes and heart wide open.*

above *Packaging in Japan: a bento box purchased at the train station demonstrating even fast food can be creative and beautiful.*

opposite *A collection of items in a bird's nest exploring creativity through nature.*

Finding your stream of creativity

There are so many myths around creativity that are absolute nonsense. These myths hold you and everyone else back from their creative potential. Thinking someone was 'born creative', or that you cannot be creative unless you are making 'art', is not only unhelpful but also false.

Everyone is already so creative in ways they haven't considered. The way you dress, colour code a spreadsheet, arrange things on a shelf or converse with strangers – these are all creative processes. But because these are all things that come naturally, it is easy to hold onto the myth that creativity is filled with angst and effort. You need to let go of these thoughts and expand your ideas about how to access your creativity.

Instead of thinking of creativity as being 'artistic', widen your understanding of creativity to include:

- considering problems using a lateral approach
- communicating effectively
- parenting
- cooking and serving meals
- planning your mornings, evenings and in-between

Discovering your existing creativity

This is a simple task to involve your awareness. Once you acknowledge where you're creative, you'll find affirmations everywhere. Journal where you are thinking laterally, solving problems in new ways and appreciating beauty and the world around you. Nothing is too small.

Ask the close people in your life, and those you view as creative, to share with you the ways in which they see your creativity. Note these down too.

Now you have a list – short or long, it doesn't matter. The key is to amplify these areas. Remember that you're already creative, so how can you acknowledge and heighten that experience? Previously you may have been blind to it, but now really dive into your thinking. Unpack it, discover and, most importantly, own that you are a creative person.

right *On a retreat in India, I handpainted affirmations for our students with watercolours, a simple yet rewarding process.*

Finding your new creativity

New creative paths are always exciting, and they proliferate once you start seeking them. There are a few key things to consider when enhancing creativity in your life. Note your answers to these questions in your journal:

- Are you investing time into being creative?
- Are you holding off on taking up a creative pursuit or hobby because you think it has to be fancy and complicated?
- How could you start, even if you only have limited time? Could you commit a morning per month to some free-flowing creative time?

Too often we put off creativity because we think we have to wait until there is more time, or more money or a dedicated space. We can create anything anywhere when we put our minds to it.

below *This is the workspace of Atelier Shirokumasha, a leather product company in Osaka, Japan. We fell completely in love with it as a temple of creativity!*

High-Grade Living

Breaking down creativity blocks

below left *The studio of the sculptor Brancusi in Paris, France.*

below right *Setting up Arran's creative studio after painting the entire thing white. It was such a pleasure to build the space from scratch, with tables we made ourselves and shelves our friends built for us, as well as a huge ottoman that Arran had made fifteen years earlier for his art gallery. The space held old creative projects and new work collectively in harmony.*

following pages *We often create while travelling. This is a tiny watercolour made in India, and Arran working in Byron Bay, Australia, from The Atlantic hotel. We often work from hotels, as they become our home away from home and we take our projects with us.*

Creativity is an exploration. It's about being curious and staying open to possibility in every moment. When we are feeling creatively constricted, we can feel suffocated. Creativity is about flow and expansion.

If you feel your creativity is being blocked, answer the following questions in your journal to allow creativity to move through you again.

- How can you apply your creativity to this situation?
- How can you exercise your full potential in this moment?
- How can you trust in the universe in this moment?

Do this continually until it wires into every neuron, and you will master life.

High-Grade Living

Aligning your creative spaces

When you look at the spaces where you live and work, do you find them inspiring? If not, why not? What's lacking? What could you add that would make these spaces more aligned with your creative processes?

You don't need to have a lot of – or even any – expensive art to display to make a creative space. Consider items that are rich in personal meaning rather than monetary value, such as photos with friends, paintings by family members, or the odd postcard from your travels. Even a collection of images from Pinterest can be taped to the wall, refreshed and replaced every few months to inspire your work and living spaces.

The key is to not think, 'Oh, I can't have visually creative things around me as I don't have a big art budget.' You don't need one. Apply creativity to the very process of building creative spaces.

above and opposite, top left My dear friend and artist Anna-Wili Highfield touching up a sculpture she made for Arran from paper many years ago that needed a facelift, in the middle of our lounge room during a barbecue, as creativity can be attended to at any time. It doesn't have to confined to the studio.

opposite, bottom left Our lounge room at the pink house that would often double as an art room.

opposite, bottom right Installing a piece by artist Poppy Kural in The Broad Place Paddington School, in Sydney, Australia. The hall was a celebration of creativity from friends and exhibitions we had held or been in ourselves.

Enhancing your creative spaces

Go from room to room and reduce or remove anything that doesn't align with your concept of high-grade living. With careful consideration, add to your spaces any visuals such as artwork, posters and pictures that inspire you.

Finding inspiration

Think of the universe as a flow of creativity. However, it certainly isn't going to visit someone who sits around frustrated, waiting for inspiration to strike.

Instead, are you visiting creativity? Staying inspired and immersing yourself in others' ideas and processes is important for creative flow. Often people who work specifically in creative fields are not filling their creative tanks.

There is a world of inspiring imagery and creative people out there. It's just about keeping your eyes open and being receptive. Remember not to use other people's creations as a trigger for jealousy. This is contractive thinking. You want to make sure that your interaction with inspiration is expansive.

Make visiting art galleries and bookstores, seeing live music, going to the cinema and attending book or poetry readings a priority. Immersing yourself in the creative minds of others is very rewarding, as it can break up the ingrained neural pathways and divert the mind into another world.

Source inspiration from everywhere. Find images you love on social media and start copying them as a painting or drawing. Note interesting ways to frame a photo, or the way light has been used to make the image more dynamic on social media platforms. Start experimenting. You don't need a fancy or expensive camera, or a decade of training, to take a great photo.

If food lights you up, then read cookbooks for ideas and watch brilliant cooking shows. Find beautiful documentaries on inspiring people approaching creativity in new ways to feed your mind with new possibilities.

If gardens are your creative outlet, then make some special trips to famous gardens and really soak up the environment. Journal, sketch or photograph everything you enjoy about the experience.

Discovering your own creative excursions

Create a list of creative places you have been meaning to visit. If you need help, tourist guidebooks can be a surprisingly good resource for the city you live in, with so many incredible things to do that you might have forgotten about or not even been aware of as a resident.

Once a fortnight, plan a creative excursion. It might be a gallery visit or a talk at the gallery by an artist on a certain night. Perhaps it's booking tickets to see a band or going to a foreign film festival for a weekend mid-morning viewing. The possibilities are endless. Even just an hour in a venue dedicated to creative output can feel restorative and can shift your creative thinking.

below *A tiny coffee house in Tokyo, Japan, the ultimate city for creative excursions.*

Creative journaling

Creative journaling is a great way to unleash your thoughts onto a page. It's not a diary, but rather a stream of consciousness. You can use old diaries, notebooks or whatever is lying around – it can even be the back of an envelope. Don't get precious, just write.

We feel that creative journaling is best done in the morning, when you are fresh from waking or meditating. The mind is more at ease and unburdened by a day's worth of decision-making, and you can tap more deeply into your subconscious.

Sometimes when I'm really stuck, I will pick up a book – usually the *Tao Te Ching*, or *Meditations* by Marcus Aurelius – and read a chapter, and then dissect it with my own interpretation. I find this always gets my thinking flowing, and I can usually find a link to a project or relationship, or something to be learned and implemented.

opposite *Journaling can take any form: a special book, loose pieces of paper, something you might bind together later. It can be words, but also visuals. Don't get precious, just get started.*

High-Grade Living

Creating with nature

Taoism is about being in total and utter alignment with nature. Someone who follows the Tao (pronounced 'dow') adopts an attitude of acceptance and is natural, unhurried and humble, and in tune with their own mind and body. Taoism recognises that everyone has their own rhythm, like seasons in nature. When we are rushing and not present, we fall out of alignment with these rhythms. One way to get back in tune is to incorporate nature into your creative processes.

opposite, top left *Nature is a huge source of inspiration. We made these at River Hawk Ranch in Byron Bay, Australia, as part of a retreat, using balsa wood and natural materials found on the property.*

opposite, top right *Beauty is found everywhere in nature and is so inspiring once we open our eyes to it, like these patterns left in the scribbly gums.*

opposite, bottom right *More patterns found in nature to be copied and traced.*

below *So many natural materials can be used creatively. For example, one of our workshops at River Hawk Ranch involved painting with mud.*

High-Grade Living

Discovering creativity
in nature

Being creative with nature doesn't have to involve giant flower displays like the ones you see at the florist. Plants don't need to be purchased from a store or market. Even handpicked flowers and little twigs in a small vase are beautiful.

Make a ritual of going for a walk and collecting small things along the way that you can arrange at home. Each time you glance at them on the windowsill or on your work desk, you'll be reminded of your walk and recall that creativity is a process and a practice to engage in at every turn.

Try bushwalking and look at how trees and other plants make their shapes. Look at their compositions and synergies. Draw or paint a scene to document your observations. There is so much inspiration in nature – so many colour palettes, textures and shapes.

left *Our homes have always been filled with plants, including lots of tiny vases with single-stem flowers. The more the better as far as we are concerned!*

following pages, right *This is a copalera that I made at River Hawk Ranch, in Byron Bay, Australia, after discovering them through a friend. Essentially, they are clay vessels in which to place burning embers and burn copal resin – a ritual for the senses.*

High-Grade Living

Living *zengosaidan*

Zengosaidan is a Zen expression that means placing all your efforts into each day so that you have no regrets and no need to grieve or worry about what is in the past.

It's about having nothing weighing upon you, taking responsibility and being proactive. When we apply ourselves expansively and creatively to each task, the day feels full and real, and not like a runaway train we can never quite catch up to.

Cultivating presence through creativity

It is insanely challenging to maintain single-minded focus in modern times. The good news is that we can use creativity as a brain-training tool.

Pick any type of visual art form you like, such as drawing, painting or sculpting, and commit to creating something using that particular art practice. Try carving out a small amount of time each day or week and see what develops. Working with simple lines and shapes can be helpful, as geometry seems to calm the mind.

Allow your mind to be singularly present for the task at hand, without worrying about what it will look like when you've finished. This is a creation for creativity's sake, not something you will necessarily frame at the end.

left *A dog we fell in love with at a gallery in Chelsea, New York, USA, who was utterly relaxed and present, sleeping up the wall with the art. Being relaxed is something we can all enjoy more of.*

opposite, top left *Take a moment to pause and admire the little things. We have collections of shells from our local beach, twigs, sticks and little totems to remind us to slow down and appreciate nature's creativity.*

opposite, top right *Something as simple as petals can be used to create mandalas or other patterns for a moment of appreciation in the day.*

opposite, bottom left *Books, single twigs, paintings and tiny ceramics on display at Cereal magazine's office in Bath, England, encourage you to slow down and appreciate the craft in small things.*

opposite, bottom right *If you're not confident with painting, copy favourite images from Instagram.*

High-Grade Living

Communicating creatively

Communication is one area of creativity that is frequently overlooked. We know that writing is creative, as is any form of storytelling, such as comedy. Yet we can be creative in all our forms of communication.

There are lots of ways to explore how you communicate and layer in new creative approaches. If you're an extrovert and are naturally very chatty, try to incorporate more pauses, silence and listening to mix up your communication. If you are an introvert, try speaking up and out when you might normally stay silent. Breaking our normal patterns is key to expanding the mind.

I've always considered email arduous – but then I received a few out-of-office messages from a friend who had used her email autoresponder to tell hilarious stories about why she was not answering her emails. It certainly proved that any form of communication can be creative.

Walking meetings are another wonderful discovery. You can often navigate communication much more dynamically while out in nature, on the move and breathing in fresh air. Conversation flows more easily, ideas don't seem as fixed, and when the flow does get stuck, there's always something interesting to observe.

opposite *Our 'second family', the Amos Eakins. We spend so much time immersed in discussions about art, nature, the creative process and self-development with all our kids, always including them in the conversation from a young age. Storytelling is one of the oldest forms of passing down knowledge.*

following pages *In London, England, Arran and I walk so much, hatching ideas and fleshing out our projects. The streets and parks make for a beautiful backdrop as they constantly shift with the seasons.*

High-Grade Living

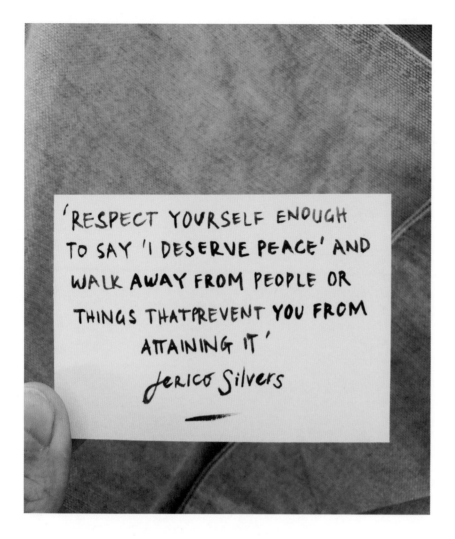

Incorporating ritual

It's a good idea to incorporate rituals into your creative processes as much as you can. You might have particular scents you love, such as incense, room sprays or candles. These can become sensory markers to set your mind up for creative work.

Music can also play a big part in creativity and ritual. Many writers say they have one or a few music tracks that they play on loop while writing. Experiment with music for various creative moments in life and see what really lights you up. You might prefer soft music or binaural beats for focused desk work, but something more energising when you're doing an activity such as cooking.

above *Handpainted notes are a brilliant ritual, gift and reminder to yourself about what's important.*

Creating ritual

Some authors can only write in hotel rooms, away from their homes. Some musicians create music on the road; some retreat into nature to let the ideas flourish.

Journal your responses to these questions about your creative expression:

- Is there a particular place where you feel more creative?
- Is there a special time of day when you feel your creativity really flows?
- Is there a particular time of day you feel very out of flow?
- When you feel creative, do you need quiet, or do you prefer music playing?
- What rituals do you already incorporate into your day to enhance your creativity? Can you subtract or add an element to experience something different?

These questions will help you understand your optimal environment for expressing creativity, if you have one. It might be at home, at work, in a park, in a studio. For me, it's wherever I can find the time – I don't get fussy about creating perfect environments, but for others, they are critical. Experiment to find what works for you.

Deepening Your Relationships

Our beliefs, ideas and assumptions about the world are reflected back at us through the relationships with people in our lives. There are countless opportunities to study these reflections, as all of us – even monks living in monasteries – must interact with others. Therefore, studying relationships is a brilliant way to begin the creative work of understanding ourselves better.

Though learning how to connect with others begins at a very young age, it's rare that we receive any formal education in connecting with ourselves. So we have a dilemma: relationships with others can be a gateway to understanding ourselves on a more intimate level, but we need to understand ourselves if we are to relate successfully with others. This chapter is all about gaining that clarity.

As you think about your relationships and interactions with other people, remember how counterproductive it is to compare their lives to your own. We all fall prey to the same things at some point or another: gossip, worrying about what other people think, wanting more love and approval, or being gripped by our egos and feeling guilt and shame. It's time for us to have a greater understanding of our own humanity so that we can be more compassionate, kind, loving and generous with others in our lives.

Understanding yourself

Living a high-grade life means being utterly clear about who you are, and you do this through creativity and consciousness. We often see the world only through our own worldview, which has been built on our individual experience. It stands to reason there are as many worldviews as there are people in the world, and this is also one of the reasons why relating can be so challenging. We have all had the experience of thinking, 'Why can't this person just *get it*?' when what we really mean is 'Why can't they see what I see?' Which, in essence, is near impossible.

Clarity is your rudder in a storm, directing you. Creativity helps you sail more gracefully in any situation. Consciousness helps you to be more in flow and engage with everything more expansively. You also have your values, which are always present and can truly calm and ground you in every situation.

High-Grade Living

High-Grade Living

Questioning yourself

Begin to get some clarity on where your life is right now by following the prompts below in your journal. There are no right or wrong answers here. It's important to just write what first comes into your mind. You may find it difficult to answer one or some of these questions. That's completely normal and means you just need more clarity in those areas of your life.

- The qualities I really admire in others are...
- The areas in my life where I see my relationships flourish are...
- I find my relationships usually flounder in areas such as...
- Ways in which I can see myself blocking flow in my relationships include...
- Ways in which I am destructive in my relationships are...
- Ways in which I am aligned with my higher-grade self – the things I am proud of – in relationships are...

previous pages *Marley and Arran greeting the sunrise at the pink house in Palm Beach, Sydney, Australia, as was our daily ritual. In Vedic philosophy, it's an auspicious time of day to say, 'Jai Surya' (which means 'praise to you, sun') as a welcome to the source of life on earth.*

opposite, top left *A sign from our travels in a little window serves as a pertinent reminder.*

opposite, top right *Journaling and documenting is such an important ritual for understanding yourself better.*

opposite, bottom *Having friendships where you can invite questioning and honesty is one of the fastest tracks to evolving and growing, individually and together.*

'When your values are clear to you, making decisions becomes easier.'

—Roy E. Disney

Understanding your values

Our values are our guides through life; they help us to understand ourselves. Values also act as anchors, grounding and stabilising us. Understanding your values is key to living an authentic life. They are what steady you in the storm of modern living, allowing you to be true to yourself.

You can also think of your values as the markers on the map that help you navigate the ocean of your life. Though we may find alignment in some areas, there will always be times when we find ourselves out of alignment with where we want to be.

Living out your values consciously is the path to a more enriched life. Our values are learned and adopted from many different areas in our life. They may have been pushed on us when we were young, learned in school or experienced in our careers or in our relationships. It might take a while to work out which values are really true to you, and which you have adopted as a result of your experiences with others. You'll discover that, generally speaking, your favourite people will have similar values to yours. It's because of your aligned values that you connect. You will also discover that when someone in your life has no values that align with yours, you'll probably find relating to them quite tricky.

If you aren't clear on who you are, you can drift from your path. Knowing and aligning yourself with your values delivers clarity in the greatest form. This is where we are going to start. Then we will move on to some other amazing exercises that can help you gain even greater clarity.

opposite, top The tall trees of Big Sur, California, USA, strong and powerful, ancient and wise.

following pages, right A note above my desk to remind me to check in and not use my ego as a cover for living an intention-led and authentic life.

Deepening Your Relationships   169

Finding your values

It can be hard to identify your values, but this activity should help. Get a piece of paper and write down the names of three people you admire deeply. You don't have the know them personally, but you need to have a strong sense of what you admire in them.

Write down what it is you admire about them. You might use words such as truth, creativity, integrity, honesty, kindness, compassion or generosity. Find the top five words that stand out to you on your list, that send chills down your spine and make your heart pound. Write these five words on a fresh page. You now have a list of your values. You can tweak, delete and add as you like. But you'll find the core of your values is there, as your subconscious knows what they are. This exercise is so helpful because when you put aside the question 'What are my values?' and enter a space of admiring another instead, your heart will talk to you.

You can update this list every 3–6 months, as your thinking can shift as you evolve.

opposite *Little collections of nature, reminding us to return to our true natural selves.*

Assessing life alignment

Using your list, ask yourself what areas of your life align with these values and what areas are out of alignment. At the moment, just bring these into your awareness. You don't need to change or act on anything right away.

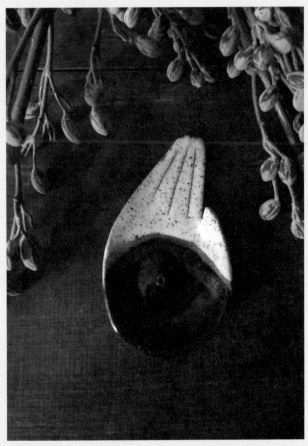

Seeking clarity

When you find yourself in a situation that throws you utterly off balance, leaving you confused and upset, you can come back to your values to provide clarity on what to do and how to respond. Here are some simple questions you can ask yourself:

- What are my core values that I want to live by daily, not just as concepts but also as a path to exploring my truth?

- Are my actions taking me away from my values? How could I better align to my values in this situation?

- Is my current thinking blocking me from my values? If so, what thoughts do I need to let go of in order to be more aligned?

- Is there a value I can fully embody in this moment to empower me?

These questions will help you find clarity, so use them as often as you need. Journal about your values and your processes to align with them, and you will learn even more about yourself, leading to greater resilience.

top *Arran in Naoshima, Japan, pausing for a moment of stillness and contemplation.*

bottom *We have always encouraged a connection to nature with Marley, and a sense of exploration and intrigue wherever we are in the world.*

Living your values

Begin a daily inventory of moments when you were truly aligned and living your values. This exercise hard-wires this alignment in the brain. Your values shouldn't be left as a dusty list on a piece of paper, but should become actions you live by and through every day.

High-Grade Living

top and bottom *Arran and I are always documenting, exploring, collecting resources and capturing moments to share at The Broad Place.*

opposite *Hiking and getting a different perspective always seems to make an impression on us in our lives, helping broaden our minds.*

High-Grade Living

Deepening Your Relationships

The power of words

Sadly, we all know the experience of saying something we regret, or emailing something in a moment of anger. Words can hurt deeply but can also uplift us, help us connect with people and express love.

Don Miguel Ruiz's book *The Four Agreements* outlines two concepts that form the foundation for high-grade communication: 'Be impeccable with your word' and 'Don't make assumptions'. Beautiful advice, but easier said than done.

When you begin to look more deeply into how you are communicating, ask yourself these questions: Do you look in the mirror and find things about yourself that you don't like? Would you say to a child what you're telling yourself? Do you occasionally speak negatively about someone to others? Would you say the same things if a child were listening?

It is very easy to become involved in a negative conversation about another person. Gossip is the unnecessary discussion of other people's lives, and taking part can impact you emotionally and physically. Think of the way you stand or move when participating in these discussions. Your body may be closed off or turned away as you concentrate on the nature of your conversation. Now think of the way you move or stand when taking part in a positive conversation. You not only move more lightly, but also feel lighter and more at peace.

'Great minds discuss ideas;
average minds discuss events;
small minds discuss people.'

—Henry Thomas Buckle

No more toxic talk

Everyone deserves our respect. When we gossip about someone and judge their actions and behaviour, we are failing to give them that respect.

Answer the following questions to help you reflect on the way you speak about others:

- Who do you find you gossip with the most?
- How do you feel while gossiping and immediately after?
- Think of a recent conversation involving gossip about someone and imagine that the person in question had been in the room. Would you still have spoken the same way?
- Think about the concept of a high-grade life. Does your understanding of what this concept means inspire you to change the way you communicate?
- What key things are you going to focus on in your communication in the future?

Now set a target of not gossiping for a month. Setting a no-gossip challenge will really lift the lid and shine some light onto where and when these negative discussions take place. The real difficulty lies in conversing with people who gossip a lot. One option is to explain your vow to avoid gossip, though that risks offending the person, who may not be aware that they are gossiping. A less confrontational approach is to simply stay neutral and not further the conversation.

At the beginning, middle and end of your no-gossip challenge, finish the following sentences in your journal:

- When I speak positively about someone I know, I feel...

- When I speak negatively about someone I know, I feel...

- When I speak positively about someone I don't know, I feel...

- When I speak negatively about someone I don't know, I feel...

- When I speak negatively about others, my body feels...

- When I speak positively about others, my body feels...

- The particular people I often discuss are...

- I discuss these people because...

- A particular friend or colleague whom I notice I fall into gossip with is...

- I can reframe my gossiping into something more conscious and positive by...

High-Grade Living

Setting a daily intention

Intentions are powerful tools that the brain can wire as truths over time. They are like little paths for us to walk down that eventually turn into a road for the brain to fly down easily.

Write down the following statement in your journal and then read it aloud regularly. It is a very powerful commitment.

I commit to the highest-grade communication and will only engage in conversation that increases my authenticity.

Communicating honestly

When your mind jumps to an assumption, ask yourself, 'Do I actually know this to be true?' Get used to always challenging your biases and prejudices. Use your journal to reflect on these questions:

- Is there someone in your life you are always making assumptions about?

- Are you aware of why you do this?

- What would it look like for you if you stopped assuming and expecting?

- Do you ever expect someone to 'read your mind' and blame them when they don't?

- How do you feel when communication isn't clear to you?

- Do mixed messages from someone else make you feel strong and empowered or nervous and belittled?

- Can you elevate your communication to be clearer?

above *A stunning installation on the art island of Japan, Teshima, where you enter and hold silence for your whole visit, and where you find you can communicate deeply within yourself, so poetic and quiet is the space.*

opposite *Our rescue dog Toofy, who teaches us so much about love and having an open heart, and does it all wordlessly.*

Deepening Your Relationships

High-Grade Living

above left *Lantana is actually a weed in Australia, yet so pretty, and anything can be appreciated.*

above right *The pink house Palm Beach, Sydney, Australia, taught us to love the things that mattered. We had no belongings of our own, and a squidgy small space, but within that we learnt to love the owls at night, the visiting birds, meals eaten outdoors, seeing every sunrise and sunset, the visiting snakes, the kookaburras that would steal our food, and time spent together as a family.*

Finding love in all things

Love everybody. Seems like a tall order, doesn't it? Yet almost every spiritual teacher has this as the cornerstone of their teaching: love everyone, love everything. So how do you go about achieving it, especially when people can frustrate you deeply?

Spiritual leader Ram Dass taught that you can love someone's soul even if you're not a fan of their personality. It's easy to get caught up in your dislike or hatred of people's personalities or differences. You need to remember to love other people at their core, as fellow human beings and someone's son or daughter.

Letting love flow

Love is the foundation of many of the qualities and experiences we consider positive, such as kindness, compassion, generosity and gratitude.

Answering the questions below in your journal will help you understand how you can let your love flow and strengthen your connection with others.

- Where in your life are you currently very loving?

- Where in your life do you find love challenging or limited?

- Where in your relationships do you find love flows easily?

- Are you holding back from giving love due to a particular perception? Can you let go of this idea to allow love to flow more easily?

- Can you begin the work of loving yourself more deeply so that you can share more love for others?

left *Our two senior rescue dogs, who have taught us an immense amount about love and its capacity to heal.*

opposite *When you open yourself to love, you find it everywhere. Can you spot the love heart?*

Reaching for connection

Ram Dass used the mantra 'Ram', which means 'God', repeated continuously to connect to a more conscious energy. Try saying this mantra to yourself whenever you think to. It doesn't have to refer to a religious god, although it can; it can represent whatever you feel a connection with, whether it's consciousness, the universe, nature, your heart or a person in your life whom you love. It's beneficial to have a connection outside of the mind's negativity for the times when you need it, and this mantra works beautifully, repeated gently to yourself as you go about your day.

above *Lovers at a temple in Kyoto, Japan.*

opposite *Me in India, where I find I am the most open-hearted and connected due to the intensity of the experiences I always have there.*

High-Grade Living

Deepening Your Relationships

High-Grade Living

Notes

Diving into Meditation

p. 31   Quote by Ram Dass: 'Less is More', *RamDass.org*, 14 November 2014, <ramdass.org/less-is-more>.

p. 38   'In 2011, researchers at Massachusetts General Hospital reported the findings of a study on the impact of meditation on the brain': Massachusetts General Hospital, 'Mindfulness meditation training changes brain structure in eight weeks,' *ScienceDaily*, 21 January 2011, <sciencedaily.com/releases/2011/01/110121144007.htm>.

p. 38   'There is also evidence that regular meditation practice can keep a person's brain up to twenty years younger compared to the brains of people who don't meditate': Matthew Johnstone and Michael Player, *StressLess: Proven Methods to Reduce Stress, Manage Anxiety and Lift Your Mood*, Pan Macmillan Australia, Sydney, 2019.

p. 38   'More than 35 million people in the US alone report having practised meditation': Karen Kaplan, 'More Americans are meditating now than were just 5 years ago', *The Seattle Times*, 21 November 2018, <seattletimes.com/nation-world/more-americans-are-meditating-now-than-were-just-5-years-ago>.

p. 52   Quote by Thich Nhat Hanh: *Peace Is Every Step: The Path of Mindfulness in Everyday Life*, Bantam Books, New York, 1992.

Deepening Your Relationships

p. 181   Quote by Henry Thomas Buckle: Charles Stewart, *Haud Immemor: Reminiscences of Legal and Social Life in Edinburgh and London 1850–1900*, William Blackwood & Sons, Edinburgh and London, 1901, p. 33.

Curious for More Inspiration?

Meditation, the Mind and Spiritual Knowledge

A Monk's Guide to a Clean House and Mind, Shoukei Matsumoto, Particular Books, 2018

Apprenticed to a Himalayan Master: A Yogi's Autobiography, Sri M., Magenta Press, 2010

Awareness, Anthony de Mello, Image, 1990

Be As You Are: The Teachings of Sri Ramana Maharshi, Sri Ramana Maharshi, edited by David Godman, Penguin Random House India, 1991

Become What You Are, Alan Watts, Shambhala Publications, 1995

Becoming Bodhisattvas: A Guidebook for Compassionate Action, Pema Chodron, Shambhala Publications, 2018

Be Here Now, Ram Dass, Lama Foundation, 1971

Braving the Wilderness: The Quest for True Belonging and the Courage to Stand Alone, Brené Brown, Random House, 2017

Bringing Home the Dharma: Awakening Right Where You Are, Jack Kornfield, Shambhala Publications, 2011

Dropping Ashes on the Buddha: The Teachings of Zen Master Seung Sahn, Seung Sahn, Grove Press, 1994

Ego Is the Enemy, Ryan Holiday, Portfolio, 2016

Emptiness Dancing, Adyashanti, Sounds True Inc, 2006

Everyday Tao: Living with Balance and Harmony, Deng Ming-Dao, HarperOne, 1996

Falling into Grace: Insights on the End of Suffering, Adyashanti, Sounds True Inc, 2011

Freedom from the Known, Jiddu Krishnamurti, HarperOne, 1975

How to Cook Your Life: From the Zen Kitchen to Enlightenment, Dogen, Shambhala Publications, 2005

In the Realm of Hungry Ghosts: Close Encounters with Addiction, Gabor Maté, Knopf Canada, 2008

Jewel in the Lotus: Deeper Aspects of Hinduism, Sri M., Magenta Press, 2011

Love for Imperfect Things: How to Accept Yourself in a World Striving for Perfection, Haemin Sunim, Penguin Books, 2018

Maharishi Mahesh Yogi on the Bhagavad-Gita: A New Translation and Commentary with Sanskrit Text (Chapters 1–6), Maharishi Mahesh Yogi, Penguin Books, 1990

Meditations, Marcus Aurelius

Meditations of Maharishi Mahesh Yogi, Maharishi Mahesh Yogi, Bantam Books, 1973

Mindfulness in Plain English, Henepola Gunaratana, Wisdom Publications, 1992

No Time to Lose: A Timely Guide to the Way of the Bodhisattva, Pema Chodron, Shambhala Publications, 2005

On Meditation: Finding Infinite Bliss and Power Within, Sri M., Penguin Random House India, 2019

Paths to God: Living the Bhagavad Gita, Ram Dass, Harmony, 2005

Polishing the Mirror: How to Live from Your Spiritual Heart, Ram Dass, Sounds True Inc, 2013

Power, Freedom, and Grace: Living from the Source of Lasting Happiness, Deepak Chopra, Amber-Allen Publishing, 2006

Stillness Speaks, Eckhart Tolle, New World Library, 2003

Super Brain: Unleashing the Explosive Power of Your Mind to Maximize Health, Happiness, and Spiritual Well-Being, Deepak Chopra and Rudolph E. Tanzi, Harmony, 2012

Tao Te Ching, Lao Tzu, translated by Stephen Mitchell, Quarto UK, 2015

Tao: The Watercourse Way, Alan Watts, Pantheon Books, 1975

The Brain That Changes Itself: Stories of Personal Triumph from the Frontiers of Brain Science, Norman Doidge, Penguin Books, 2007

The Five Invitations: Discovering What Death Can Teach Us About Living Fully, Frank Ostaseski, Flatiron Books, 2017

The Inside-Out Revolution: The Only Thing You Need to Know to Change Your Life Forever, Michael Neill, Hay House, 2013

The Mahabharata: A Modern Rendering, Ramesh Menon, Rupa Publications, 2004

The Power of Now: A Guide to Spiritual Enlightenment, Eckhart Tolle, New World Library, 1997

The Purpose of Life, Torkom Saraydarian, TSG Publishing Foundation, 1991

The Ramayana: A Modern Translation, Ramesh Menon, HarperCollins India, 2010

The Space Within: Finding Your Way Back Home, Michael Neill, Hay House, 2016

The Spirit of Zen: A Way of Life, Work, and Art in the Far East, Alan Watts, Grove Press, 1994

The Surrender Experiment: My Journey into Life's Perfection, Michael A. Singer, Harmony, 2015

The Teachings of Tempu: Practical Meditation for Daily Life, H. E. Davey, Michi Publishing, 2013

The Tibetan Book of Living and Dying, Sogyal Rinpoche, HarperCollins, 1992

The Unfettered Mind: Writings of the Zen Master to the Sword Master, Takuan Soho, translated by William Scott Wilson, Shambhala Publications, 2012

The Untethered Soul: The Journey Beyond Yourself, Michael A. Singer, Harbinger, 2007

The Upanishads, translated by Eknath Easwaran

The Wisdom of No Escape: How to Love Yourself and Your World, Pema Chodron, Shambhala Publications, 1991

The Yogi's Roadmap, Bhavani Silvia Maki, CreateSpace, 2013

Transcending the Levels of Consciousness: The Stairway to Enlightenment, David R. Hawkins, Veritas Publishing, 2006

Twilight Goddess: Spiritual Feminism and Feminine Spirituality, Thomas Cleary, Shambhala Publications, 2002

Wanting Enlightenment Is a Big Mistake: Teachings of Zen Master Seung Sahn, Seung Sahn, Shambhala Publications, 2006

When Things Fall Apart: Heart Advice for Difficult Times, Pema Chodron, Shambhala Publications, 1996

Wherever You Go, There You Are: Mindfulness Meditation in Everyday Life, Jon Kabat-Zinn, Hyperion, 1994

Who Would You Be Without Your Story?, Byron Katie, Hay House, 2008

The Body and Wellness

Ashtanga Yoga: Practice and Philosophy, Gregor Maehle, New World Library, 2007

Ayurveda: A Life of Balance: The Complete Guide to Ayurvedic Nutrition and Body Types with Recipes, Maya Tiwari, Healing Arts Press, 1994

Ayurveda and the Mind: The Healing of Consciousness, David Frawley, Lotus Press, 1997

Ayurveda Secrets of Healing: Complete Ayurvedic Guide to Healing Through Pancha Karma Seasonal Therapies, Diet, Herbal Remedies and Memory, Maya Tiwari, Lotus Press, 1995

Ayurveda: The Science of Self-Healing, Vasant Lad, Lotus Press, 2004

Balance Your Hormones, Balance Your Life: Achieving Optimal Health and Wellness through Ayurveda, Chinese Medicine, and Western Science, Claudia Welch, Da Capo Lifelong Books, 2011

Chasing the Sun: The New Science of Sunlight and How It Shapes Our Bodies and Minds, Linda Geddes, Wellcome Collection, 2019

Conscious Eating, Gabriel Cousens, North Atlantic Books, 2000

Healing with Whole Foods: Asian Traditions and Modern Nutrition, Paul Pitchford, North Atlantic Books, 1993

Jivamukti Yoga: Practices for Liberating Body and Soul, Sharon Gannon and David Life, Random House USA, 2002

Nourishing Traditions: The Cookbook That Challenges Politically Correct Nutrition and the Diet Dictocrats, Sally Fallon, New Trends Publishing, 2009

Nourishing Wisdom: A Mind-Body Approach to Nutrition and Well-Being, Marc David, Harmony, 1994

One Simple Thing: A New Look at the Science of Yoga and How It Can Transform Your Life, Eddie Stern, North Point Press, 2019

Perfect Health: The Complete Mind/Body Guide, Deepak Chopra, Harmony, 1990

The Body Keeps the Score: Brain, Mind, and Body in the Healing of Trauma, Bessel van der Kolk, Viking Press, 2014

The Macrobiotic Way: The Definitive Guide to Macrobiotic Living, Michio Kushi and Stephen Blauer, Avery, 2004

The Tao of Inner Peace, Diane Dreher, Plume, 2000

Women's Power to Heal: Through Inner Medicine, Maya Tiwari, Mother Om Media, 2007

Creativity and Thinking

A Whole New Mind: Why Right-Brainers Will Rule the Future, Daniel H. Pink, Riverhead Books, 2006

Big Magic: Creative Living Beyond Fear, Elizabeth Gilbert, Riverhead Books, 2015

Make the Impossible Possible: One Man's Crusade to Inspire Others to Dream Bigger and Achieve the Extraordinary, Bill Strickland, Currency, 2009

Predatory Thinking: A Masterclass in Out-Thinking the Competition, Dave Trott, Pan Macmillan, 2013

Rethink: The Way You Live, Amanda Talbot, Murdoch Books, 2012

Surrender: A Journal for My Daughter, Joshua Yeldham, Pan Macmillan, 2016

The Art of Asking: How I Learned to Stop Worrying and Let People Help, Amanda Palmer, Little, Brown Book Group, 2014

Inspiration

Consolations: The Solace, Nourishment and Underlying Meaning of Everyday Words, David Whyte, Many Rivers Press, 2015

Graceful, Seth Godin, New Word City, 2010 (eBook only)

Illusions: The Adventures of a Reluctant Messiah, Richard Bach, Delacorte Press, 1977

I Thought It Was Just Me: Women Reclaiming Power and Courage in a Culture of Shame, Brené Brown, Gotham Books, 2007

My Stroke of Insight: A Brain Scientist's Personal Journey, Jill Bolte Taylor, Penguin Books, 2009

Return of the Rishi: A Doctor's Story of Spiritual Transformation and Ayurvedic Healing, Deepak Chopra, Houghton Mifflin, 1991

Status Anxiety, Alain de Botton, Hamish Hamilton, 2004

The Art of Travel, Alain de Botton, Hamish Hamilton, 2002

The Desire Map: A Guide to Creating Goals with Soul, Danielle LaPorte, Sounds True Inc, 2014

The Four Agreements: A Practical Guide to Personal Freedom, Don Miguel Ruiz, Amber-Allen Publishing, 1997

The Gifts of Imperfection: Let Go of Who You Think You're Supposed to Be and Embrace Who You Are, Brené Brown, Hazelden Publishing, 2010

The Prophet, Kahlil Gibran, Rupa & Co, 2010

The Seven Spiritual Laws of Success: A Practical Guide to the Fulfillment of Your Dreams, Deepak Chopra, New World Library, 1994

Thrive: The Third Metric to Redefining Success and Creating a Life of Well-Being, Wisdom, and Wonder, Arianna Huffington, Harmony, 2014

Truck Nest – A Record: Nine Years in the Making, Truck Furniture (Tokuhiko Kise and Hiromi Karatsu), Shueisha, 2012

When Breath Becomes Air, Paul Kalanithi, Random House, 2016

Cooking

Breakfast, Lunch, Tea: The Many Little Meals of Rose Bakery, Rose Carrarini, Phaidon, 2005

Japanese Farm Food, Nancy Singleton Hachisu, Andrews McMeel Publishing, 2012

Jerusalem: A Cookbook, Sami Tamimi and Yotam Ottolenghi, Ebury Publishing, 2012

Living Ahimsa Diet: Nourishing Love & Life, Maya Tiwari, Mother Om Media, 2012

Nigel Slater's Real Food, Nigel Slater, HarperCollins UK, 1998

Plenty, Yotam Ottolenghi, Ebury Publishing, 2010

The Japanese Grill: From Classic Yakitori to Steak, Seafood, and Vegetables, Harris Salat and Tadashi Ono, Random House USA, 2011

The Kitchen Diaries, Nigel Slater, Fourth Estate, 2005

Acknowledgements

We would like to deeply thank all our students, without whom The Broad Place wouldn't even exist. We would both like to thank our families, for their endless support of the work we do. Thank you to our friends for all their patience, as this process has not been an easy one, and they have been there for us with their huge hearts the whole way. I would love to send gratitude to all my teachers across the decades, who have guided me and taught me well. Thank you to the whole team at Thames & Hudson, especially Paulina de Laveaux, who learnt to meditate with us many years back and truly held the vision of what we were trying to create with such clarity and belief. I owe so much to Brigid James, for her endless conversations and deep dives into the shape of the book as our editor, and her shaping it into what it is. And thank YOU for engaging with the philosophy of high-grade living, and living a heart-led life with more clarity, for it is with this intention that we hope the world becomes a more graceful and engaged place to live within.